# Phrase**Guide**

## JAPANESE

**With menu decoder, survival guide and two-way dictionary**

**Thomas Cook** Publishing

www.thomascookpublishing.com

# Survival guide...............49

# Emergencies....................59

# Dictionary........................63

# Quick reference...............95

## How to use this guide

The ten chapters in this guide are colour-coded to help you find what
you're looking for. These colours are used on the tabs of the pages
and in the contents on the previous page and above.

For quick reference, you'll find some basic expressions on the inside
front cover and essential emergency phrases on the inside back
cover. There is also a handy reference section for numbers,
measurements and clothes sizes at the back of the guide.

Front cover photography © Tohoku ColorAgency/Getty Images
Cover design/artwork by Jonathan Glick
Photos: Jonathan Baker-Bates (p35), Dreamstime.com [Aaleksander (p58),
Maksym Bondarchuk (p47), Reed Daigle (p48), Everjean (p15), Ramon Grosso
(p17), Heavyj (p16), Tan Jace (p32), Kuan Chong Ng (p46), Patrick Macdonald
(p57), Chris Mccooey (p56), Navarone (p59), Radu Razvan (pp19, 33, 34, 50
& 60), Anette Romanenko (p22), Szefei (p7) and Ryu Yamazaki (p25)], Naomi
Hasegawa/BigStockPhoto.com (p8), Angelune des Lauriers (p44), Midorisyu
(p52) and Peter Van den Bossche (p40).

**Produced by The Content Works Ltd**
Aston Court, Kingsmead Business Park, Frederick Place
High Wycombe, Bucks HP11 1LA
www.thecontentworks.com
Design concept: Mike Wade
Layout: Alison Rayner
Text: Charles Pringle
Editing: Paul Hines
Proofing: Monica Guy & Mieko Suzuki
Editorial/project management: Lisa Plumridge

**Published by Thomas Cook Publishing**
A division of Thomas Cook Tour Operations Limited
Company registration No: 3772199 England
The Thomas Cook Business Park, 9 Coningsby Road
Peterborough PE3 8SB, United Kingdom
Email: books@thomascook.com, Tel: +44 (0)1733 416477
www.thomascookpublishing.com

ISBN-13: 978-1-84848-103-9

First edition © 2009 Thomas Cook Publishing
Text © 2009 Thomas Cook Publishing

Project Editor: Maisie Fitzpatrick
Production/DTP: Steven Collins

Printed and bound in Italy by Printer Trento

# Introduction

Japanese is spoken by about 128 million people in Japan, along with sections of the populations of Korea, Taiwan, China and the Philippines. Spoken Japanese is not difficult but it reflects Japanese society in that it is hierarchical, and at its advanced level it is fairly complex. Honorific language is used when respect is called for and informal language is used between friends and peers; in most cases, a form of neutral or polite language is spoken. This guide simplifies Japanese to help you handle most situations you are likely to encounter on a visit to Japan. So don't be shy – give it a try.

# The basics

The Japanese have never been shy about importing things and adapting them to suit their own needs. Nowhere is this commendable practical and labour-saving openness to outside influences more apparent than in the language, which, in its present form, actually represents a rich confluence of linguistic ingredients. In this aspect, if in very few others, it has a lot in common with English.

During the sixth century, as the country opened up to Chinese and Korean ideas, the Japanese adopted the Chinese writing system known as *kanji*, along with a large number of Chinese words. This was but a prelude to their flinging wide open their cultural doors to the Indo-European languages, for they subsequently embraced a host of words from English (for example, *wāpuro* = word processor), French (*ankōru* = "encore"), German (*baito* = part-time work, from "*Arbeit*") and many other languages. They even developed a syllabic character set, *katakana*, to distinguish loan words from Japanese words that are either written in *kanji* or *hiragana*, another syllabic character set.

Due to the fact that written Japanese uses those three different character sets, reading the language can be extremely challenging. Moreover, as Japanese has every syllable clearly pronounced, these imported loan words can be difficult to understand. However,

## Loan words

Many adopted words are pronounced exactly as they are written, which can sometimes make them incomprehensible. The word *ta-ren-to*, for example, comes from the English word "talent" and, ironically, means a television personality.

## Pronunciation

The pronunciation of Japanese is relatively simple because the syllables are always pronounced exactly the same. Each syllable starts with a consonant and ends with a vowel. In this guide, long vowels are indicated by a macron above the letter.

making yourself understood in terms of verbal communication is not at all difficult and, once armed with this book, will be an enjoyable exercise that will endear you to one and all. Just as a footnote, there is no need to employ what might be termed a 1970s sitcom approximation of a Japanese accent.

## Grammar

Japanese sentence structure is different from that of English. For instance, instead of our "I saw a dog", the word order in the Japanese system would be "A dog I saw". Another important element of Japanese is the role played by "particles" – short words which link phrases and tell you what kind of sentence you are hearing. Take the sentence *densha no kippu arimasu ka*? ("Do you have a train ticket?"). A direct translation would be "train ticket have?". The particle *ka* is used to indicate a question, implying "do you...?" – without it, the sentence would simply mean "I have a train ticket". The particle *no* links the train (*densha*) and ticket (*kippu*) together. The verb (or, as you will remember from those happy days spent frolicking nimbly in the groves of academe, "doing word"), comes at the end of the sentence. Unless you want to hold court in a noodle bar, wowing the locals with Wildean witticisms communicated in such deathless Japanese that you eventually leave the venue accompanied by the sound of chopstick applause, you really don't need to worry too much about the grammar – just try out some of the phrases in this book and you'll pick up the general sense of things in no time.

## Basic conversation

| | | |
|---|---|---|
| Goodbye | さようなら | *Sayōnara* |
| Yes | はい | *Hai* |
| No | いいえ | *Iie* |
| Please | お願いします | *Onegai shimasu* |
| Thank you | ありがとうございます | *Arigatō gozaimasu* |
| You're welcome | どういたしまして | *Dō itashimashite* |
| Sorry | すみません。<br>　ごめんなさい | *Sumimasen.*<br>　*Gomen nasai* |
| Excuse me<br>　(apology) | すみません | *Sumimasen* |
| Excuse me<br>　(to get attention) | すみません | *Sumimasen* |
| Excuse me<br>　(to get past) | すみません | *Sumimasen* |
| Do you speak<br>　English? | 英語を話しますか？ | *Eigo o*<br>　*hanashimasu ka?* |
| I don't speak<br>　Japanese | 日本語を話すことがで<br>　きません | *Nihongo o hanasu*<br>　*koto ga dekimasen* |
| I speak a little<br>　Japanese | 日本語を少しを話し<br>　ます | *Nihongo o sukoshi*<br>　*hanashimasu* |
| What? | 何ですか？ | *Nan desu ka?* |
| I understand | 分かります | *Wakarimasu* |
| I don't understand | 分かりません | *Wakarimasen* |
| Do you understand? | 分かりますか？ | *Wakarimasuka?* |
| I don't know | 知りません | *Shirimasen* |
| I can't | できません | *Dekimasen* |
| Can you please<br>　speak more slowly? | もう少しゆっくり言っ<br>　て下さい | *Mō sukoshi yukkuri*<br>　*itte kudasai* |
| Can you please<br>　repeat that? | もう一度言って下さい | *Mō ichi do*<br>　*itte kudasai* |

## Made in Japan?

The Japanese predilection for customising English words or phrases leads to fumbles such as the cosmetics company whose marketing slogan is the deathless "For Beautiful Human Life".

# Greetings

Japanese has no word for "hello"; instead greetings reflect the time of day. Before noon, for example, use *ohayō gozaimasu*; in the afternoon say *Konnichiwa*; and in the evening *Konbanwa*. When you are introduced to someone for the first time, however, use *hajimemashite* followed by your name (*watashi wa* [name] *desu*). Japanese people greet each other with a bow, the junior person bowing lower than the senior, and rarely make eye contact. There are a number of ways of saying goodbye. The best known is *sayōnara*, but *shitsurei shimasu* ("I'm about to be impolite") is also used. Younger people are more casual and use the terms *jya ne* or *mata ne*.

## Meeting someone

| Good morning | おはようございます | *Ohayō gozaimasu* |
| Good afternoon | こんにちは | *Konnichiwa* |
| Good evening | こんばんは | *Konbanwa* |
| | | |
| Sir/Mr | さん | *San* |
| Madam/Mrs | さん | *San* |
| Miss | さん | *San* |
| | | |
| How are you? | お元気ですか？ | *Ogenki desu ka?* |
| Fine, thank you | はい、おかげさまで | *Hai, okagesama de* |

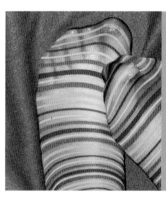

## Small gift, clean socks

It's wise to bring a few small gifts from your own country in case you are invited somewhere in Japan. Be sure to wear pristine socks: you could be asked to remove your shoes.

## Small Talk

| My name is... | 私は ... です | *Watashi wa ... desu* |
| What's your name? | お名前は、何ですか？ | *Onamae wa nan desu ka?* |
| I'm pleased to meet you! | お会いできて光栄です | *Oai dekite kōei desu* |
| How do you do? | 初めまして、どうぞよろしく | *Hajimemashite. Dōzo yoroshiku* |
| How do you do? (reply to above) | 初めまして、こちらこそよろしく | *Hajimemashite. Kochira koso yoroshiku* |
| Where are you from? | お国は、どちらですか？ | *Okuni wa dochira desu ka?* |
| I am from England | イギリスから来ました | *Igirisu kara kimashita* |
| Do you live here? | ここにすんでいますか？ | *Koko ni sunde imasu ka?* |

| | | |
|---|---|---|
| This is a great country | ここは素晴らしい国です | *Koko wa subarashii kuni desu* |
| This is a great city/town | ここは素晴らしい町です | *Koko wa subarashii machi desu* |
| I am staying at (the Prince Hotel) | 私は（プリンスホテル）に宿泊しています | *Watashi wa (Purinsu Hoteru) ni shukuhaku shite imasu* |
| I'm just here for the day | 私は今日だけここにいます | *Watashi wa kyō dake koko ni imasu* |
| I'm in (Tokyo) for a weekend | 私は週末（東京に）います | *Watashi wa Shūmatsu Tokyo ni imasu* |
| I'm in (Tokyo) for a week | 私は1週間（東京に）います | *Watashi wa isshūkan (Tokyo) ni imasu* |
| How old are you? | あなたは何歳ですか？ | *Anata wa nan sai desu ka?* |
| I'm... years old | 私は … 歳です | *Watashi wa ... sai desu* |

## Family

| | | |
|---|---|---|
| This is my husband | 私の夫です | *Watashi no otto desu* |
| This is my wife | 私の妻です | *Watashi no tsuma desu* |
| This is my partner | 私のパートナーです | *Watashi no pātonā desu* |
| This is my boyfriend/girlfriend | 私の彼/彼女です | *Watashi no kare/kanojo desu* |
| I have a son | 私は息子がいます | *Watashi wa musuko ga imasu* |
| I have a daughter | 私は娘がいます | *Watashi wa musume ga imasu* |

### Strop ye not
The Japanese are calm and reserved. Nothing looks worse to them than an angry foreigner ranting and raving.

| I have a grandson | 私は孫（男の子）がいます | *Watashi wa mago-musuko ga imasu* |
| I have a granddaughter | 私は孫娘がいます | *Watashi wa mago-musume ga imasu* |
| Do you have children? | 子供がいますか？ | *Kodomo ga imasu ka?* |
| Do you have grandchildren? | 孫がいますか？ | *Mago ga imasu ka?* |
| I don't have children | 私は子供がいません | *Watashi wa kodomo ga imasen* |
| Are you married? | 結婚していますか？ | *Kekkon shite imasu ka?* |
| I'm single | 私は独身です | *Watashi wa dokushin desu* |
| I'm married | 私は結婚しています | *Watashi wa kekkon shite imasu* |
| I'm divorced | 私は離婚しています | *Watashi wa rikon shiteimasu* |
| I'm widowed | 私は未亡人です | *Watashi wa mibōjin desu* |

## Saying goodbye

| Goodbye | さようなら | *Sayōnara* |
| Good night | お休みなさい | *Oyasuminasai* |
| Sleep well | よくお休みください | *Yoku oyasumi kudasai* |
| See you later | また後で | *Mata ato de* |
| Have a good trip! | よいご旅行を! | *Yoi goryokō o!* |
| It was nice meeting you | お会いできて良かったです | *Oai dekite yokatta desu* |
| All the best | 幸運を祈ります | *Kōun o inorimasu* |
| Have fun! | 楽しんでください! | *Tanoshinde kudasai!* |
| Good luck! | 幸運を祈ります！ | *Kōun o inorimasu!* |
| Keep in touch | 連絡を取り合いましょう | *Renraku o toriaimashō* |
| My address is... | 私の住所は … です | *Watashi no jūsho wa ... desu* |
| What's your address? | 住所は何ですか？ | *Jūsho wa nan desu ka?* |
| What's your email? | メールアドレスは何ですか？ | *Mēru adoresu wa nan desu ka?* |
| What's your telephone number? | 電話番号は何番ですか？ | *Denwa bangō wa nanban desu ka?* |

# Eating Out

As well as familiar dishes such as sushi
and *sukiyaki*, Japan offers a staggering
array of foods served in a diverse range
of eateries. At the bottom end of the
scale are the *yatai* (street stalls) and the
top are the *kaiseki ryōri*, restaurants
that serve Japanese haute cuisine. You
will also find restaurants that serve both
typical Japanese dishes and a wide range
of international food. The country's
fifteen different regional cuisines offer
a tremendous range, from the Arctic
seafood dishes of Hokkaido in the
north to the exotic pork-based meals
of Okinawa. Moreover, Japan has four
distinct seasons, so look out for special
seasonal dishes.

## Introduction

The Japanese love eating out. For breakfast, most cafés offer *mōningu sābisu* (morning service), which usually consists of toast, an egg, a small salad and tea or coffee. At lunchtime most restaurants offer good-value meals consisting of soup, salad, a main dish and rice. Many also provide a *tabehōdai* (all-you-can-eat) or a *nomihōdai* (all-you-can-drink) fixed price option in the evening. Drinking is wildly popular in Japan.

| | | |
|---|---|---|
| I'd like a table for two | 二人用のテーブルをお願いします | *Futariyō no tēburu o onegaishimasu* |
| I'd like a sandwich | サンドイッチをお願いします | *Sandowichi o onegaishimasu* |
| I'd like a coffee | コーヒーをお願いします | *Kōhī o onegaishimasu* |
| I'd like a (black) tea | 紅茶をお願いします | *Kōcha o onegaishimasu* |
| I'd like a tea with milk | ミルクティーをお願いします | *Miruku tī o onegaishimasu* |
| Do you have a menu in English? | 英語のメニューはありますか？ | *Eigo no menyū wa arimasuka?* |
| The bill, please | お勘定をお願いします | *O-kanjō o onegaishimasu* |

### You may hear...

| | | |
|---|---|---|
| *Tabako o suimasu ka?* | タバコを吸いますか？ | *Smoking or non-smoking?* |
| *Nani ni nasaimasu ka?* | 何になさいますか？ | *What are you going to have?* |

### Civil service

The Japanese go the extra mile to provide service to diners. While most menus are in Japanese, many eateries have plastic food models of the meals in the window or photos in the menus.

## Okonomiyaki

*Okonomiyaki* is a type of savoury pancake that consists of various ingredients grilled in a batter. You select them from a menu and cook the pancake on a hotplate in the center of the table.

# The cuisines of Japan

## Regional specialities

Fish and seafood – cooked or eaten raw – feature in a wide variety of Japanese dishes. Restaurants serving *soba* (buckwheat noodles), *udon* (wheat noodles) and *ramen* (Chinese noodles) are ubiquitous, and so are *tonkatsu-ya* that serve breaded pork cutlets. Diverse hotpot dishes are served in traditional establishments, where *yakitori* (grilled chicken) is also popular. *Unagi* (chargrilled eel) is definitely worth trying.

**Signature dishes** (see the menu decoder for more dishes)

| | | |
|---|---|---|
| 散らし寿司 | *Chirashi zushi* | Sashimi on sushi rice |
| すき焼き | *Suki yaki* | Hotpot of beef and vegetables |
| しゃぶしゃぶ | *Shabu shabu* | Sliced beef in boiling stock |
| ちゃんこ鍋 | *Chanko nabe* | Hotpot eaten by sumo wrestlers |
| うなぎ | *Unagi* | Grilled eel on a bed of rice |
| そば | *Soba* | Buckwheat noodles in sauce |
| うどん | *Udon* | Wheat flour noodles in sauce |
| おでん | *Oden* | Egg, vegetable and fish cake hotpot |
| 寄せ鍋 | *Yose nabe* | Seafood, vegetable and chicken stew |

**Not for the squeamish**
*Natto* (written as 納豆) is a dish that the Japanese like to challenge foreigners to eat. Made from fermented soy beans, it has a strong pungent odour and a very sticky texture.

| | | |
|---|---|---|
| 天ぷら | *Tempura* | Deep-fried seafood and vegetables |
| とんかつ | *Tonkatsu* | Fried breaded pork cutlet |
| 串揚げ | *Kushi age* | Deep-fried, skewered seafood and veg |
| 刺身 | *Sashimi* | Raw fish in soy sauce and wasabi |
| 握り寿司 | *Nigirizushi* | Raw fish on sushi rice |
| 巻き寿司 | *Makizushi* | Raw fish in rice and seaweed |
| 手巻き寿司 | *Temakizushi* | As above but rolled in a cone |

## Nagasaki

The cuisine of Nagasaki blends the best foods from Japan, China and the West. Nagasaki *chanpon* is Chinese noodles, pork, squid, oysters, shrimp, clams, bean sprouts, cabbage and edible fungi. Another favourite, *shippoku-ryori*, consists of an assortment of dishes severed on a large lacquered table.

| | | |
|---|---|---|
| チャンポン | *Chanpon* | Noodles with meat, seafood and veg |
| 皿うどん | *Sara udon* | Thick meaty sauce on noodles |
| カステラ | *Kasutera* | Sponge cake |

## Kyoto

There are three main styles. *Kaiseki-ryōri* consists of one soup, sashimi, *yakimono* (grilled dish) and *nimono* (boiled dish), but additional dishes are often included. Similar food is served in the formal, banquet-style *Honzen-ryōri*. The food is carefully arranged on small tables and strict eating rules apply.

| | | |
|---|---|---|
| 湯豆腐 | *Yudōfu* | Tofu dipped in sauce |
| さば寿司 | *Saba zushi* | Vinegared mackerel on rice |
| 湯葉 | *Yuba* | Fresh or dried soya milk skin |

## Hokkaido

The cuisine of Hokkaido features fresh fish, vegetables, high-quality meat and *ramen* (noodles). It offers a variety of *nabemono* (hotpots) such as *Ishikari-nabe*, which consists of salmon, salmon roe and assorted vegetables. Seafood rice bowls, *Kaisendon*, are unique to Hokkaido.

| | | |
|---|---|---|
| るいべ | *Ruibe* | Sliced raw fish in soy sauce |
| ジンギスカン | *Jingisukan* | Grilled mutton and vegetables |
| 三瓶汁 | *Sanpei jiru* | Miso soup with salmon and veg |

### From import to national dish

To most people *tempura* (seafood and vegetables deep-fried in batter) is a typical Japanese dish, but in fact it was introduced to Japan in the 16th century by Portuguese missionaries.

## Kagoshima

Pork is a major ingredient here, and it is cooked in a variety of ways. *Tonkotsu* (spare ribs) is an extremely distinctive dish: the meat is stewed slowly in a broth of *shōchū* (distilled alcohol), *kurosatō* (black sugar) and miso until it practically falls off the bone.

| 角煮 | *Kakuni* | Cubes of pork in broth |
| 豚骨 | *Tonkotsu* | Stewed pork belly and ribs |

## Slap-up slurping

The Japanese love to slurp their food, particularly noodles. This can be a shock to Westerners, so brace yourself!

## Tokyo

Tokyo has a diverse traditional cuisine based on fish and seafood from Tokyo Bay and vegetables from the fertile plain that surrounds the city. The best-known form of sushi is known as *Edo-mae-zushi* in Japan because it originated in Edo (the former name for Tokyo). Tsukudani consists of fish or seafood boiled in soy sauce over a long period.

| うなぎの蒲焼 | *Unagi no kabayaki* | Charcoal-grilled sauce-basted eel |
| やながわなべ | *Yanagawa nabe* | Loach with burdock root and egg |
| もんじゃ焼き | *Monja yaki* | Savoury, slightly runny pancake |

## Seasonal Cooking

Unlike most of East Asia, Japan has four distinct seasons, which exert a great influence on the cuisine. Traditionally the ingredients used changed with the season, so there was a set pattern of meals throughout the year. Even today, although nowadays food technologies prolong the life of many ingredients, the Japanese tend to consider certain dishes seasonal.

## Spring

There is a wide variety of edible vegetation available in the spring. Bamboo shoots, *takenoko*, are dug up as soon as they appear above ground, and they are eaten in various dishes. *Sansai* or wild mountain vegetables are plentiful in the mountains and around the paddy fields. And certain fish and seafood, such as sea bream, Spanish mackerel and clams are delicious at this time of the year.

| たけのこご飯 | *Takenoko gohan* | Bamboo shoots in rice |
| すまし汁 | *Sumashi jiru* | Clam and trefoil soup |
| 山菜めし | *Sansai meshi* | Rice with wild mountain veg |

## Summer

Summer is hot and humid in Japan, so salt and vinegar appear in quite a few summer dishes. Raw *maguro* (tuna) and *katsuo* (bonito), slightly flavoured with vinegar, are sashimi favourites, and grilled *ayu* (sweet fish) is also very popular. Cold noodles, Chinese as well as Japanese, are often eaten at lunch.

| 枝豆 | *Edamame* | Salted green soybeans |
| しぎやき | *Shigiyaki* | Halved egg plant with miso |
| そーめん | *Sōmen* | Thin white noodles eaten cold |

## Not tipped but taxed

Tipping isn't really practised in Japan, but table taxes will relieve you of troublesome change.

### Yatai

Every visitor to Japan should eat at least once at a *yatai* (street stall). Most specialise in one dish such as *ramen*, *okonomiyaki* or *oden* (hotpot), but some offer a much greater selection that includes grilled chicken, fish and *sashimi* as well as vegetable and tofu dishes.

## Autumn

Autumn serves up a banquet of fish, fruit and vegetables – wild as well as cultivated – in dishes that are either cooked or eaten raw. *Saba* (mackerel) and *Sanma* (saury) are delicious at this time of the year as are the edible fungi, such as the highly priced *matsutake*. The *ginnan*, the nut of the ginko tree, is also an autumnal favourite.

| 茶碗むし | Chawan mushi | Egg custard with seafood and meat |
| 石焼芋 | Ishiyaki imo | Sweet potato baked over hot stones |
| 栗ご飯 | Kurigohan | Boiled rice with sweet chestnuts |

## Winter

Root vegetables feature in many dishes during the winter, especially in the *nabemono* (hotpots usually cooked at the table), and so do leeks and *hakusai* (Chinese cabbage). There are also some unusual fish, such as the *ankō* (angler fish) and the potentially deadly *fugu* (swellfish), which claims a few lives every year. Oysters are also eaten raw or cooked.

| ちり鍋 | Chiri nabe | White fish hotpot with leafy vegetables |
| あんきも | Ankimo | Monkfish liver in a miso dressing |
| 松前焼き | Matsumae yaki | Oysters grilled on *kombu* (kelp) |

## Wine, beer & spirits

There are two alcoholic drinks that every visitor should try: *nihon-shū* (rice wine) and *shōchū*. The former is drunk either heated (*atsu-kan*) from a small ceramic cup or cold from a wooden box. *Shōchū* is distilled from potatoes or grain and is generally quaffed straight.

## You may hear...

| | | |
|---|---|---|
| *Nani ni nasaimasu ka?* | 何になさいますか？ | What would you like to have? |
| *Sore wa ikaga desu ka?* | それはいかがですか？ | How would you like it? |
| *Kōri iri desu ka, nuki desu ka?* | 氷入りですか、抜きですか | With or without ice? (in drinks) |
| *Wain wa reizō soretomo shitsuon desu ka?* | ワインは冷蔵それとも室温ですか？ | Cold or room temperature? (for wine) |

## Snacks & refreshments

There are cafés everywhere in Japan, but it is definitely worth visiting a *chashitsu* (traditional tea house) and trying the tea ceremony. Popular snacks include *manju* (dumpling filled with sweet bean paste) and *senbei* (rice crackers).

### Don't eat meat?

For a city of its size, Tokyo is remarkably short of exclusively vegetarian restaurants. However, many restaurants have enough veggie meals on the menu to satisfy even the most herbivorous guest.

## Vegetarians & special requirements

| | | |
|---|---|---|
| I'm vegetarian | 私はベジタリアンです | *Watashi wa bejitarian desu* |
| I don't eat... | ... を食べません | *... o tabemasen* |

| I don't eat meat | 肉を食べません | *Niku o tabemasen* |
| I don't eat fish | 魚を食べません | *Sakana o tabemasen* |
| Could you cook something without meat in it? | それに肉を入れずに何か料理できますか | *Sore ni niku woirezuni nanika ryori dekimasu ka?* |
| What's in this? | なにが入っていますか | *Nani ga haitte imasu ka?* |
| I'm allergic to... | 私は … アレルギーです | *Watashi wa ...arerugī desu* |
| I'm allergic to beans | 私は豆アレルギーです | *Watashi wa mame arerugī desu* |

## Children

| Are children welcome? | 子供は入ってもいいですか | *Kodomo wa haitte mo ii desu ka?* |
| Do you have a children's menu? | 子供のメニューはありますか | *Kodomo no menyū wa arimasu ka?* |
| What dishes are good for children? | どの料理が子供向きですか | *Dono ryōri ga kodomo muki desu ka?* |

### Dining with children

Most restaurants in Japan are fairly comfortable with children. The best places for them to eat, however, are the so-called family restaurants that serve mainly western dishes with a few popular Japanese or Chinese dishes also thrown in.

# Menu decoder

## Essentials

| | | |
|---|---|---|
| Breakfast | 朝御飯（あさごはん） | *Asa gohan* |
| | 朝食（ちょうしょく） | *Chō shoku* |
| Lunch | 昼御飯（ひるごはん） | *Hiru gohan* |
| | 昼食（ちゅうしょく） | *Chu shoku* |
| Dinner | 晩御飯（ばんごはん） | *Ban gohan* |
| | 夕食（ゆうしょく） | *Yū shoku* |
| Cover charge | 席料/カバーチャージ | *Seki ryō/kabāchāji* |
| Vat included | 消費税込み | *Shōhizei komi* |
| Service included | サービス料込み | *Sābisu ryō komi* |
| Credit cards (not) accepted | クレジットカード使用可（不可） | *Kurejitto kādo shiyō ka (huka)* |
| Dessert | デザート | *Dezāto* |
| Dish of the day | 本日の料理 | *Honjitu no ryōri* |
| Local speciality | ご当地特産品 | *Gotōchi tokusanhin* |
| Set menu | セットメニュー | *Setto menyu* |
| A la carte | 一品料理 | *Ippin ryōri* |
| Tourist menu | 旅行者用メニュー | *Ryokōsha yō menū* |
| Wine list | ワインリスト | *Wain risuto* |
| Drinks menu | ドリンクメニュー | *Dorinku menyu* |
| Snack menu | 軽食メニュー | *Keishoku menyu* |

### Sticky moments
Never stick your chopsticks in a bowl of rice, and never transfer food from your chopsticks to someone else's. These are both funeral rites.

## Methods of preparation

| | | |
|---|---|---|
| Baked | 焼き | *Yaki* |
| Boiled | 茹で | *Yude* |
| Braised | 蒸し煮 | *Mushini* |
| Breaded | パン粉をまぶした | *Panko o mabushita* |
| Deep-fried | 揚げ | *Age* |

| Fresh | 生 | *Nama* |
|---|---|---|
| Fried | 焼き/フライ | *Yaki/furai* |
| Fried egg | 目玉焼き | *Medama yaki* |
| Fried shrimp | エビフライ | *Ebi furai* |
| Frozen | 冷凍 | *Reitō* |
| Frozen food | 冷凍食品 | *Reitō shokuhin* |
| Grilled/broiled | 焼き | *Yaki* |
| Marinated | マリネ | *Marine* |
| Mashed | マッシュ | *Masshu* |
| Poached | ポーチド | *Pōchido* |
| Raw | 生 | *Nama* |
| Roasted | 焼き/ロースト | *Yaki/rōsuto* |
| Salty | 塩辛い | *Shiokarai* |
| Sautéed | 炒めた | *Itameta* |
| Smoked | 燻製 | *Kunsei* |
| Spicy (hot) | 辛い | *Karai* |
| Steamed | 蒸し | *Mushi* |
| Stewed | 煮込み | *Nikomi* |
| Stuffed | 詰め物 | *Tsumemono* |
| Sweet | 甘い | *Amai* |
| Rare | レア | *Re-a* |
| Medium | ミディアム | *Midīam* |
| Well done | ウェルダン | *Uerudan* |

### Nice lunch box!
*Ekiben* are boxed lunches sold on trains and stations all over Japan. Every region features its local specialities.

## Common food items

| Beef | 牛肉 | *Gyū niku* |
|---|---|---|
| Chicken | 鳥肉 | *Tori niku* |
| Turkey | 七面鳥 | *Shichimennchō* |
| Lamb | ラム肉 | *Ram niku* |
| Pork | 豚肉 | *Buta niku* |
| Fish | 魚 | *Sakana* |
| Seafood | 魚介類 / 海鮮料理 | *Gyokai rui/ kaisen ryōri* |
| Tuna | 鮪 | *Maguro* |

**Mealtime manners**
The correct way to eat is to sit with a straight back and transfer food to your mouth with chopsticks. Bowls usually fit in your hand and you can lift them up if that helps.

| | | |
|---|---|---|
| Beans | 豆 | *Mame* |
| Cheese | チーズ | *Chīzu* |
| Eggs | 卵 | *Tamago* |
| Lentils | レンズ豆/<br>ひら豆 | *Renzu mame/<br>hira mame* |
| Pasta/noodles | パスタ/ヌードル | *Pasuta/nūdoru* |
| Rice | ご飯 | *Gohan* |
| Aubergine | なす | *Nasu* |
| Cabbage | キャベツ | *Kyabetsu* |
| Carrots | にんじん | *Ninjin* |
| Cucumber | きゅうり | *Kyūri* |
| Garlic | にんにく | *Nin niku* |
| Mushrooms | マッシュルーム | *Masshurūmu* |
| Olives | オリーブ | *Orību* |
| Onion | 玉ねぎ | *Tama negi* |
| Potato | じゃが芋/ポテト | *Jaga imo/poteto* |
| Red/green pepper | 赤ピーマン / ピーマン | *Aka pīman/pīman* |
| Tomato | トマト | *Tomato* |
| Vegetables | 野菜 | *Yasai* |
| Bread | パン | *Pan* |
| Oil | 油 | *Abura* |
| Olive oil | オリーブオイル | *Orību oiru* |
| Pepper | コショウ/胡椒 | *Koshō/koshō* |
| Salt | 塩 | *Shio* |
| Vinegar | 酢 | *Su* |
| Soy sauce | 醤油 | *Shōyu* |
| Cake | ケーキ | *Kēki* |
| Cereal | シリアル | *Shiriaru* |
| Cream | 生クリーム | *Nama crīmu* |
| Fruit | フルーツ/果物 | *Furūtsu/kudamono* |
| Ice cream | アイスクリーム | *Aisukurīmu* |
| Milk | ミルク | *Miruku* |
| Tart | タルト | *Taruto* |

## Popular sauces

| 醤油 | *Shōyu* | Soy sauce |
| てんつゆ | *Tentsuyu* | Tempura sauce |
| わさび | *Wasabi* | Japanese horseradish |
| ケチャップ | *Kechappu* | Ketchup |
| テリヤキ | *Teriyaki* | Teriyaki sauce |

## Starters

| 本日の前菜 | *Hon jitsu no zensai* | Today's appetizer |
| サラダ | *Sarada* | Salad |
| オードブル | *Ōdoburu* | Hors d'œuvre |
| 漬物 | *Tsukemono* | Japanese pickles |

## Soups

| みそ汁 | *Miso shiru* | Miso soup |
| 本日のスープ | *Hon jitsu no sūpu* | Today's soup |
| コンソメ | *Konsome* | Consommé |
| ポタージュスープ | *Potāju sūpu* | Potage soup |
| わかめスープ | *Wakame sūpu* | Seaweed soup |

## Second course dishes

| ビーフシチュー | *Bīfu shichū* | Beef stew |
| ビーフステーキ | *Bīfusuteki* | Beefsteak |
| サーロインステーキ | *Sāroin sutēki* | Sirloin steak |
| 豚しょうが焼き | *Buta shōga yaki* | Pork with ginger |

## Japanese dishes

| 寿司 | *Sushi* | Sushi |
| 散らし寿司 | *Chirashi zushi* | Sashimi on rice |
| 握り寿司 | *Nigiri zushi* | Raw fish on rice |
| 巻き寿司 | *Maki zushi* | Rolled sushi |
| 手巻き寿司 | *Temaki zushi* | Fish in a seaweed cone |
| 刺身 | *Sashimi* | Fish in soy sauce |
| すき焼き | *Suki yaki* | Beef and veg hotpot |
| しゃぶしゃぶ | *Shabu shabu* | Beef dipped in stock |
| 寄せ鍋 | *Yose nabe* | Seafood or vegetable hotpot |
| ちゃんこ鍋 | *Chanko nabe* | Sumo wrestlers' hotpot |
| おでん | *Oden* | Seafood broth |
| 天ぷら | *Tempura* | Tempura |
| うなぎ | *Unagi* | Grilled eel |

| 焼肉 | *Yaki niku* | Grilled meat |
| そば | *Soba* | Buckwheat noodles |
| うどん | *Udon* | Wheat flour noodles |
| とんかつ | *Tonkatsu* | Pork cutlet |
| 串揚げ | *Kushi age* | Deep-fried seafood & vegetables |

## These boots were made for filling

When you really need to fill up, head for a restaurant or hotel offering a *Baikingu* (all-you-can-eat-buffet). For a set price you can nosh without restriction in an allotted time (usually two hours).

## Side dishes

| サラダ | *Sarada* | Salad |
| 枝豆 | *Edamame* | Green soybeans |
| お新香 | *Oshinko* | Pickled vegetables |
| 春巻き | *Haru maki* | Spring rolls |
| なす田楽 | *Nasu dengaku* | Aubergine with sweet miso |
| ポテトフライ | *Poteto furai* | French fries |

## Desserts

| アイスクリーム | *Aisukurīmu* | Ice cream |
| ケーキ | *Kēki* | Cake |
| チョコレートパフェ | *Chokorēto pafe* | Chocolate sundae |
| バナナパフェ | *Banana pafe* | Banana sundae |
| フルーツサラダ | *Furūtsu sarada* | Fruit salad |

## Drinks

| コーヒー | *Kōhī* | Coffee |
| アイスコーヒー | *Aisukōhī* | Iced coffee |
| カフェオーレ | *Kafe ōre* | Milky coffee |
| エスプレッソ | *Esupuresso* | Espresso |

| 紅茶 | *Kōcha* | Black tea |
| レモンティ | *Remon tī* | Tea with lemon |
| ミルクティ | *Miruku tī* | Tea with milk |
| アイスティ | *Aisu tī* | Iced tea |
| お茶 | *Ocha* | Green tea |
| ミルク | *Miruku* | Milk |
| ココア | *Kokoa* | Cocoa |
| オレンジジュース | *Orenji jūsu* | Orange juice |
| りんごジュース | *Ringo jūsu* | Apple juice |
| 水 | *Mizu* | Water |
| ビール | *Bīru* | Beer |
| 生ビール | *Nama bīru* | Draft beer |
| 瓶入りビール | *Bin bīru* | Bottled beer |
| ウイスキー | *Uisukī* | Whisky |
| 水割り | *Mizuwari* | Whisky with water |
| ウイスキーソーダ | *Uisukī soda* | Whisky with soda |
| オンザロック | *Onzarokku* | On the rocks |
| ウォッカ | *Wokka* | Vodka |
| ブランディ | *Burandē* | Brandy |
| 赤ワイン | *Aka wain* | Red wine |
| 白ワイン | *Shiro wain* | White wine |
| 日本酒 | *Nihon shū* | Japanese sake |
| お酒 | *Osake* | Japanese sake |
| 焼酎 | *Shōchū* | Potato hooch |

## Tourist traps
Some restaurants advertise set menu Japanese cuisine in traditional surroundings, served by English-speaking staff; great, but you'll need to take out a mortgage to pay for the drinks!

## Snacks

| 枝豆 | *Edamame* | Green soybeans |
| お新香 | *Oshinko* | Pickled vegetables |
| キムチ | *Kimuchi* | Spicy pickled white cabbage |
| しらすおろし | *Shirasu Oroshi* | Baby sardines with grated radish |
| おつまみ | *Otsumami* | Japanese snacks |

# Shopping

Oh, fortunate indeed the shopper in Japan! The country has some of the best shops on the planet, and malls like Roppongi Hills and Midtown that house a blistering array of designer boutiques. You will also find vivid markets flogging everything from antiques and traditional souvenirs to second-hand or designer clothes. In Akihabara, which is known as "Electric Town", there are hundreds of electronics shops offering everything from the latest computers, cameras and audiovisual equipment to second-hand goods. While prices tend to be high, there are great bargains in the discount stores (some of which also offer duty-free shopping).

## Essentials

| | | |
|---|---|---|
| Where can I buy...? | ...はどこで買えますか？ | ... wa doko de kaemasu ka? |
| I'd like to buy... | ...を買いたい | ... o kaitai |
| Do you have...? | ...は、ありますか？ | ... wa arimasu ka? |
| Do you sell...? | ...は、売っていますか？ | ... wa utteimasu ka? |
| I'd like this | ...が欲しいです | ... ga hoshī desu |
| I'd prefer... | ...のほうが好きです | ... o konomimasu |
| Could you show me...? | ...を見せてください | ... o misete kudasai |
| I'm just looking, thanks | ちょっと見ているだけです | Chotto mite iru dake desu |
| How much is it? | これはいくらですか？ | Kore wa ikura desu ka? |
| Could you write down the price? | 値段を紙に書いてください | Nedan o kami ni kaite kudasai |
| Do you have any items on sale? | セール品はありますか？ | Sēru mono wa arimasu ka? |
| Could I have a discount? | 割り引きしてくれませんか？ | Waribiki shite kuremasen ka? |
| Nothing else, thanks | それで全部です | Sore de zenbu desu |
| Do you accept credit cards? | クレジットカードは使えますか？ | Kurejitto kādo wa tsukaemasu ka? |
| It's a present: could I have it wrapped, please? | プレゼント用に、つつんでもらえますか？ | Purezento yō ni, tsutsunde moraemasuka? |
| Could you post it to...? | ここから…に郵送できますか？ | Koko kara ... ni yūsō dekimasu ka? |

## To haggle or not to haggle?

Haggling is not customary: prices are fixed and sales staff would think it strange if you tried for a discount. However, street markets such as Ameyoko are suitable bargaining arenas.

| Can I exchange it? | 交換したいんですが | *Kōkan shitain desu ga* |
| I'd like to return this | 返品したいんですが | *Henpin shitain desu ga* |
| I'd like a refund | 返金してもらいたいんですが | *Henkin shite moraitain desu ga* |

## Shopping for souvenirs

One of the best places to shop for typical Japanese souvenirs is Nakamise, a street in front of Asakusa's Sensōji temple. You'll find rice crackers, traditional confectionery, toys, fans, paper umbrellas, dolls, T-shirts, old kimonos and woodblock prints.

## Local specialities

The traditional crafts of Japan provide excellent souvenirs. Paper products, or *washi*, such as origami paper, notebooks and fans are light and inexpensive. You will also find great lacquerware (*shikki*) in prices ranging from reasonable to outrageous. Kimonos and *yukata* (a simple informal kimono) are also easy to pack and carry and are inexpensive.

| Can you recommend a shop selling local specialities? | 名産品を買える良いお店を教えてください | *Meisanhin o kaeru yoi omise o oshiete kudasai* |
| What are the local specialities? | 名産品は何ですか？ | *Meisanhin wa nan desu ka?* |
| What should I buy from here? | ここで何を買ったら良いですか？ | *Koko de nani o kattara yoi desu ka?* |
| Is this good quality? | この品質は良いですか？ | *Kono hinshitsu wa yoi desu ka?* |
| Do you make this yourself? | 自分で作りましたか？ | *Jibun de tsukurimashita ka?* |
| Is it handmade? | ハンドメイドですか？ | *Hando meido desu ka?* |
| Can I order one? | ひとつ注文したいのですが | *Hitotsu chūmon shitai no desu ga* |

## Popular things to buy

Photographic equipment such as lenses and flash units as well as cameras – film-based or digital – and video equipment are popular and can be quite reasonably priced in the chain camera shops. It is also worth buying audiovisual equipment in Japan, but be sure to get an export model (those for the domestic market are designed to run on 100 V).

### Men's clothing

Buying coats, jackets and trousers can be challenging in Japan. In the case of a coat or jacket, while the chest and shoulders might fit, the arms can often be short. With trousers it is the leg that is short.

## Clothes & shoes

The Japanese are very meticulous dressers, so the quality of clothes made in the country is high. While imported designer clobber can be expensive, reasonably priced, good quality gear is the norm. Be careful when buying trousers, shirts or jackets because the leg or the arm is often shorter than in the West. Shoe sizes in Japan are measured in centimetres.

| Where is the... department? | ...売場はどこですか？ | ... uriba wa doko desu ka? |
|---|---|---|
| - clothes | - 洋服 | - yōfuku |
| - shoe | - 靴 | - kutsu |
| - women's | - 婦人 | - fujin |
| - men's | - 紳士 | - shinshi |
| - children's | - 子供 | - kodomo |
| Which floor is the...? | …は何階ですか | ... wa nankai desu ka? |
| | | |
| I'm looking for... | …を探しています | ... o sagashite imasu |
| | | |
| - a skirt | -スカート | - sukāto |
| - trousers | -ズボン | - zubon |
| - a halter top | -ホルタートップ | - horutātoppu |
| - a jacket | -上着 | - uwagi |

| - a T-shirt | -Tシャツ | - T shatsu |
|---|---|---|
| - jeans | -ジーパン | - jīpan |
| - shoes | 靴 | - kutsu |
| - underwear | -下着 | - shitagi |

| Can I try it on? (clothes) | 試着してもいいですか | Shichaku shite mo ii desu ka? |
|---|---|---|
| Can I try it on? (shoes/trousers) | はいてみてもいい ですか | Haite mo ii desu ka? |

| What size is it? | サイズはいくつで すか? | Saizu wa ikutsu desu ka? |
|---|---|---|
| My size is... | 私のサイズは…です | Watashi no size wa ... desu |

| - small | S | S |
|---|---|---|
| - medium | M | M |
| - large | L | L |

(see clothes size converter on p96 for full range of sizes)

| Do you have this in my size? | 私のサイズであり ますか? | Watashi no size de arimasu ka? |
|---|---|---|
| Where is the changing room? | 試着室はどこですか? | Shichaku shitsu wa doko desu ka? |

| It doesn't fit | サイズが合いません | Saizu ga aimasen |
|---|---|---|
| It doesn't suit me | 私に似合いません | Watashi ni niaimasen |

| Do you have a... size? | …サイズはありま すか? | ... saizu wa arimasu ka? |
|---|---|---|
| - bigger | もっと大きな | Motto ōkina |
| - smaller | もっと小さな | Motto chīsana |

## Shinjuku shopping

The plush Shinjuku skyscraper district of Tokyo contains many a classy retail outlet. Chief among these are Odakyu, a 16-floor – yes, that's 16 floors – department store and the comparatively titchy Keio (with a mere 11 levels).

| | | |
|---|---|---|
| Do you have it/ them in... | …色はありますか | ... iro wa arimasen ka? |
| - black? | 黒 | Kuro |
| - white? | 白 | Shiro |
| - blue? | 青 | Ao |
| - green? | 緑 | Midori |
| - red? | 赤 | Aka |
| Are they made of leather? | 皮製ですか？ | Kawa sei desu ka? |
| I'm going to leave it/them | やめておきます | Yamete okimasu |
| I'll take it/them | これにします | Kore ni shimasu |

← お入口 →
ENTRANCE

引
PULL

## A warm welcome
Whenever you enter a shop or restaurant in Japan you will be greeted with a cry of *Irasshaimase*, which roughly means "welcome". The way it is uttered depends entirely on the type of store.

## You may hear

| | | |
|---|---|---|
| いらっしゃいます | Irasshaimase | Welcome |
| サイズはいくつで すか？ | Saizu wa ikutsu desu ka? | What size? |
| うちにはございません | Uchi ni wa gozaimasen | We don't have any |
| 他に何かございま すか？ | Hoka ni nanika gozaimasu ka? | Anything else? |
| これは（五十）円です | Kore wa (go jū) en desu | It's (50) yen |

## Where to shop

| | | |
|---|---|---|
| Where can I find a... | ...はどこですか？ | ...wa doko desu ka? |
| - bookshop? | 本屋はどこですか？ | Honya wa doko desu ka? |
| - clothes shop? | 洋服屋はどこですか？ | Yōfukuya wa doko desu ka? |

| | | |
|---|---|---|
| - department store? | デパートはどこで すか? | *Depāto wa doko desu ka?* |
| - gift shop? | ギフトショップはどこで すか? | *Gifuto shoppu wa doko desu ka?* |
| - music shop? | 楽器屋はどこですか? | *Gakkiya wa doko desu ka?* |
| - market? | 市場はどこですか? | *Ichiba wa doko desu ka?* |
| - newsagent? (kiosk) | キオスクはどこで すか? | *Kiosuku wa doko desu ka?* |
| - shoe shop? | 靴屋はどこですか? | *Kutsuya wa doko desu ka?* |
| - stationer's? | 文房具屋はどこで すか? | *Bunbōguya wa doko desu ka?* |
| - tobacconist? | タバコ屋はどこで すか? | *Tabakoya wa doko desu ka?* |
| - souvenir shop? | お土産屋はどこで すか? | *Omiyageya wa doko desu ka?* |
| Where's the best place to buy...? | ...を買うのに一番良い 店はどこですか? | *... o kau noni ichiban ii mise wa doko desu ka?* |
| - a film | -フィルム | *- Fuirumu* |
| - an English newspaper | -英字新聞 | *- Eigo no shinbun* |
| - a map | -地図 | *- Chizu* |
| - postcards | -葉書 | *- Hagaki* |
| - a present | -プレゼント | *- Purezento* |
| - stamps | -切手 | *- Kitte* |
| - sun cream | -日焼け止め | *- Hiyake dome* |

**Hyaku-en shops**
There are thousands of *Hyaku-en* (100-yen) shops where you can purchase items such as tableware, household goods, and stationery for just that price.

## Food & markets

| Is there a supermarket nearby? | このあたりにスーパーマーケットはありますか？ | Kono atari ni sūpāmāketto wa arimasu ka? |
|---|---|---|
| Is there a market nearby? | このあたりに市場はありますか？ | Kono atari ni ichiba wa arimasu ka? |
| Can I have... | ...をお願いしたいんですが | ... o onegai shitain desu ga |
| - some bread? | - パン | - pan |
| - some fruit? | - 果物 | - kudamono |
| - some cheese? | - チーズ | - chīzu |
| - a bottle of water? | - 水をボトルでお願いします | - mizu o botoru de onegai shimasu |
| - a bottle of wine? | - ワインをボトルでお願いします | - wain o botoru de onegai shimasu |
| I'd like... of that | ...お願いしたいんですが | ... onegaishitain desu ga |
| - half a kilo | - ５００グラム | - Gohyaku guramu |
| - 250 grams | - ２５０グラム | - Nihyaku goju guramu |
| - a small/big piece | - 小さいの/大きいの | Chīsai no/ōkī no |

## Teenage heaven

Takeshita Dori in Harajuku, Tokyo, is a Mecca for Japan's teenagers. It is lined by boutiques and fast food outlets, and it is jam-packed with kids dressed as anime characters or punk rockers.

## Import & export

Before arrival, visitors have to fill out a customs declaration form. Personal effects are excluded from duty, as are three bottles of alcohol, 400 cigarettes, 100 cigars and two ounces of perfume. If you are carrying more than one million yen you must report it. There is a non-returnable five per cent consumption tax on everything purchased, except for items bought in tax-free shops.

# Getting Around

Japan is one of the easiest countries in the world to travel around. If you are moving far from Tokyo, you can either fly or take the *shinkansen* (bullet train); if you are travelling around Tokyo itself, there's a remarkably efficient network of metro, railways and buses. A variety of day passes cover the metropolitan area, one of which – Tokyo Free Kippu – is valid on all metro lines and Toei buses and streetcars. Two prepaid IC cards – Suica and PASMO – can be used on most trains, metro lines and buses in Greater Tokyo. The downside to public transport in Japan is that it can be very crowded, especially during rush hours.

## Arrival

Most visitors to Japan arrive at either Narita Airport, which serves Tokyo, or Kansai International Airport, the hub for Osaka, Kyoto and Kobe. Narita has three entry channels: one for Japanese, one for foreign residents, and one for visitors from abroad. All foreign visitors over the age of sixteen are photographed and fingerprinted. UK citizens can stay for six months without a visa.

| Where is/are the... | …どこですか？ | ... doko desu ka? |
|---|---|---|
| - luggage trolleys? | - カート | - kāto? |
| - lost luggage office? | - 忘れ物取扱所 | - wasuremono toriatsukai jo? |

| Where is/are the... | …はどこですか？ | ... wa doko desu ka? |
|---|---|---|
| - buses? | バスはどこで乗れますか？ | Basu wa doko de noremasu ka? |
| - trains? | 電車はどこで乗れますか？ | Densha wa doko de noremasu ka? |
| - car rental? | レンタカーはどこで借りれますか？ | Rentakā wa doko de kariremasu ka? |
| - exit? | 出口はどこですか？ | Deguchi wa doko desu ka? |

| How do I get to hotel...? | ホテル…にどうしたら行けますか？ | Hoteru ... ni dōshitara ikemasuka? |
|---|---|---|

| My baggage is... | 荷物が… | Nimotsu ga ... |
|---|---|---|
| - damaged | 荷物が損傷しています | Nimotsu ga sonshōshite imasu |
| - stolen | 荷物が盗まれました | Nimotsu ga nusumaremashita |

## Travelling by numbers

The complex network of subway lines crisscrossing Tokyo is actually fairly simple to navigate: the names of the lines are indicated by a colour and a letter, and the stations are numbered.

## Customs

The procedure at Japanese customs is very thorough. Nobody has the option of waltzing through the green channel; everybody has to line up and take their baggage to a customs officer who asks a few questions and then decides whether or not to peek inside the bags. Drugs and pornographic material are strictly prohibited and the penalties are severe.

| | | |
|---|---|---|
| The children are on this passport | 子供はこのパスポートです | *Kodomo wa kono pasupōto desu* |
| We're here on holiday | 観光できました | *Kankō de kimashita* |
| I'm going to... | …へ行きます | *... e ikimasu* |
| I have nothing to declare | 申告するものはありません | *Shinkoku suru mono wa arimasen* |
| Do I have to declare this? | これを申告しなければいけませんか？ | *Kore o shinkoku shinakereba ikemasen ka?* |

## Car hire

If you are planning to see the countryside, hiring a car can be a good idea; if you are only staying in the big cities, it is not. To hire and drive a car in Japan, you need an international driving licence, which you must get in your home country. One rental company, ToCoo, offers English-language support.

| | | |
|---|---|---|
| I'd like to hire a... | …をレンタルしたいんですが | *... o rentaru shitain desu ga* |
| - car | - 車 | *- Kuruma* |
| - people carrier | -ミニバン | *- Miniban* |
| with... | …付 | *...tsuki* |
| - air conditioning | - エアコン | *- Eakon* |
| - automatic transmission | - オートマチックトランスミッション（オートマ） | *- Ōtomachikku transumisshon (ōtoma)* |
| How much is that for a... | …でいくらですか？ | *... de ikura desu ka?* |
| - day? | - 一日？ | *- Ichi nichi?* |
| - week? | - 一週間？ | *- Isshū kan?* |
| Does that include... | …付ですか？ | *... tsuki desu ka?* |
| - mileage? | - 距離/マイレージ？ | *- Kyori/mairēji?* |
| - insurance? | - 保険 | *- Hoken?* |

## On the road

If you are driving in Japan, be careful! Be aware that the Japanese, while not as bad as drivers in some countries, do not follow the highway code as we know it. At any set of traffic lights, you are going to see four or five drivers risking their lives (and the lives of others) as they run a red light.

| | | |
|---|---|---|
| What is the speed limit? | 制限速度は何キロですか？ | *Seigen sokudo wa nan kiro desu ka?* |
| Can I park here? | ここに駐車しても良いですか？ | *Koko ni chūsha shite mo ī desu ka?* |
| Where is a petrol station? | ガソリンスタンドはどこですか？ | *Gasorin sutando wa doko desu ka?* |
| Please fill up the tank with... | …満タンでお願いします | *... man tan de onegai shimasu* |
| - unleaded | -無鉛の | *- Muen no* |
| - diesel | -ディーゼル | *- Dīzeru* |
| - LPG | エル・ピー・ジー | *- Eru pī jī* |

## Directions

| | | |
|---|---|---|
| Is this the road to...? | この道を行けば、…に着きますか？ | *Kono michi o ikeba, ... nitsukimasu ka?* |
| How far is it to...? | …までどれくらいありますか？ | *... made dore kurai arimasu ka?* |
| How long will it take to...? | …まで時間はどれくらいかかりますか？ | *... made jikan wa dore kukrai kakarimasu ka?* |
| Could you point it out on the map? | この地図でどこなのか教えてください？ | *Kono chizu de doko nanoka oshiete kudasai?* |

### All a bawd

Tokyo's last tramline, the Toden Arakawa-sen (*chin-chin densha*), meanders through some interesting districts. The northeastern terminus borders the famous one-time brothel quarter of Yoshiwara.

| | | |
|---|---|---|
| I've lost my way | 道がわからなくなり ました | *Michi ga wakaranaku narimashita* |
| On the right/left | 右/左に | *Migi/hidari ni* |
| Turn right/left | 右/左に曲がる | *Migi/hidari ni magaru* |
| Straight ahead | まっすぐ | *Massugu* |
| Turn around | Uターンする | *U-tān suru* |

## Buses
Buses are the perfect mode of transport in all Japanese cities. Fares are usually a fixed price and there are easily recognisable bus stops at regular intervals. A bus ride is a cheap sightseeing option.

## Public transport
Japan has probably the best and most efficient transport system in the world. Trains and buses are clean and safe and, most importantly, punctual, although they can get crowded at times. Take the subways in the cities – the system has been simplified by colour coding and numbering – and if you are travelling intercity, try the super-fast *shinkansen* (bullet train).

| | | |
|---|---|---|
| Bus | バス | *Basu* |
| Bus station | バス乗り場 | *Basu no tāminaru* |
| Train | 電車 | *Densha* |
| Train station | 駅 | *Eki* |
| I would like to go to... | …へ行きたいんです が | *...e ikitain desu ga* |
| I would like a... ticket | …の切符が欲しい んです　が | *...no kippu ga hoshīn desu ga* |
| - single | -片道切符 | - *katamichi kippu* |
| - return | -往復切符 | - *ōfuku kippu* |
| - first class | -グリーン車の切符 | - *gurīn sha no kippu* |
| - smoking/ non-smoking | -喫煙/禁煙 | - *kitsuen/kinnen* |
| What time does it leave/arrive? | 出発/到着は何時 ですか？ | *Shuppatsu/tōchaku wa nanji desu ka?* |

| | | |
|---|---|---|
| Could you tell me when to get off? | 降りる場所を教えて下さい？ | *Oriru basho o oshiete kudasai?* |

## Taxis

Taxis are readily available in Tokyo. There are ranks at all major stations and places of interest, and you can also hail taxis in the street. When you stop a cab, its left rear door will open automatically, and it will open automatically again after you have paid the fare.

| | | |
|---|---|---|
| I'd like a taxi to... | …までのタクシーをお願いします | *... made no takushī o onegaishimasu* |
| How much is it to the... | …まではいくらですか？ | *... made wa ikura desu ka?* |
| - airport? | 空港 | *Kūkō* |
| - town centre? | 都心 | *Toshin* |
| - hotel? | ホテル | *Hoteru* |
| Are there any organised tours of the town/region? | 町/地域を観光できるツアーはありますか？ | *Machi/chiiki o kankō dekiru tsuā wa arimasu ka?* |
| Where do they leave from? | どこから出発しますか？ | *Doko kara shuppatsu shimasu ka?* |
| What time does it start? | 何時に始まりますか | *Nanji ni hajimarimasu ka?* |

## Tours

The Hato Bus is one of the most popular sightseeing options for visitors to Tokyo. As well as the usual sightseeing routes – shrines, temples and gardens – there are trips combining shopping with Japanese cuisine and the city night life. A night cruise in a *yakata-bune* (small floating restaurant) while enjoying a typical Japanese meal is also a great option.

| | | |
|---|---|---|
| Do you have English-speaking guides? | 英語ガイドはいますか？ | *Eigo gaido wa imasu ka?* |
| Is lunch/tea included? | 昼食/お茶付ですか？ | *Chūshoku/ocha tsuki desu ka?* |
| Do we get any free time? | 自由時間はありますか？ | *Jiyū jikan wa arimasu ka?* |
| Are we going to see...? | ...は見れますか？ | *... wa miremasu ka?* |
| What time do we get back? | 何時にもどりますか？ | *Nanji ni modorimasu ka?* |

# Accommodation

Japan has a sophisticated, wide-ranging accommodation system, with all the big global hotel brands present in most cities. Visitors who want to sample some genuine Japanese hospitality should try a *ryokan* (traditional inn), in which guests sleep on futons on woven straw mat flooring and are served full-course Japanese meals. *Minshuku*, a cheaper version of the *ryokan*, are family-run lodgings where the service is more basic but has the personal touch. Some temples also offer accommodation and even allow visitors to participate in their services. Outside the cities, camping facilities are also available.

## Types of accommodation

Although Japan is considered an expensive country, hotels generally offer better value than in the UK. Check in is usually noon and check out 10am, but some establishments are flexible. A reservation is definitely advisable, and most booking can be done over the Internet. *Ryokans* offer full accommodation, including dinner and breakfast, whereas most other places serve only breakfast.

| I'd like to stay in... | …で泊まりたいんですが | ... de tomaritain desu ga |
|---|---|---|
| - an apartment | 短期アパート… | Tanki apāto ... |
| - a campsite | キャンプ場… | Kyanpu jō ... |
| - a hotel | ホテル… | Hoteru ... |
| - a youth hostel | ユースホステル… | Yūsuhosuteru ... |
| - a guest house | 民宿… | Minshuku ... |
| | | |
| Is it... | | |
| - full board? | 3食つきですか | San shoku tsuki desu ka? |
| - half board? | 2食つきですか | Ni shoku tsuki desu ka? |
| - self-catering? | 素泊まりですか | Sudomari desu ka? |

## Reservations

| Do you have any rooms available? | 部屋が空いていますか？ | Heya wa aite imasu ka? |
|---|---|---|
| Can you recommend anywhere else? | ほかのホテルを教えていただけますか？ | Hoka no hoteru o oshiete itadakemasu ka? |

### Love shack, baby!

"Love hotels" are found in all Japanese cities. They resemble European castles, ships or even cathedrals. If you and your partner are stuck for a place to stay, prices are reasonable.

| I'd like to make a reservation for... | ...予約したいんですが | ... yoyaku shitain desu ga |
|---|---|---|
| - tonight | 今晩… | Kon ban ... |
| - one night | 一晩… | Hito ban ... |
| - two nights | 二晩… | Futa ban ... |
| - a week | 一週間… | Isshū kan ... |

| From... (1st May) to... (8th May) | （5月）（1日）から（8日）まで | (Go gatsu) (tsuitachi) kara (yōka) made |
|---|---|---|

## Capsule hotels
The perfect solution for emergency accommodation, these compact hotels consist of sleeping capsules that contain a futon, TV, radio alarm and a reading light. Shower facilities are available.

## Room types

Facilities depend on the type of room and class of your lodging. At the bottom of the scale, a capsule hotel for single travellers, for example, you have a mattress and television. Most other hotels offer single, double and twin rooms with standard facilities, including TV, Internet connection and mini-bars. The big hotels also house restaurants and shopping arcades.

| Do you have room? | 部屋はありますか？ | Heya wa arimasu ka? |
|---|---|---|
| Do you have a ... room? | …の部屋はありますか？ | ... no heya wa arimasu ka? |
| - a single | シングル… | Shinguru ... |
| - a double | ダブル… | Daburu ... |
| - a family | ファミリー… | Famirī ... |

| with... | …付きの | ...tsuki no |
|---|---|---|
| - a cot? | 折りたたみ式ベッド… | Oritatami beddo ... |
| - twin beds? | ツインベッド… | Tsuin betto ... |
| - a double bed? | ダブルベッド… | Daburu betto ... |
| - a bath/shower? | バス/シャワー… | Basu/shawā ... |

45

| | | |
|---|---|---|
| - air conditioning? | エアコン… | *Eakon ...* |
| - Internet access? | インターネット接続… | *Intānetto setsu zoku ...* |
| Can I see the room? | 部屋を見てみてもよい ですか？ | *Heya o mite mo yoi desu ka?* |

## Ryokan
Japanese-style inns, *ryokan*, offer simple sleeping accommodation, in which guests sleep on futons, and are served traditional meals in comfortable surroundings.

## Prices

Hotels in Japan charge per person and not per room, except for the "love hotels" (see page 44), which usually only cater for couples. Anything taken from the mini-bar is automatically charged to your bill, as are telephone calls. Tipping is not expected, but there is a ten per cent service charge and a five per cent consumption tax that is sometimes included in the price.

| | | |
|---|---|---|
| How much is... | …はいくらですか？ | *...wa ikura desu ka?* |
| - a double room? | ダブルの部屋はいくら ですか？ | *Daburu no heya wa ikura desu ka?* |
| - per night? | 一晩ではいくらで すか？ | *Hito ban de wa ikura desu ka?* |
| - per week? | 一週間ではいくらで すか？ | *Isshuu kan de wa ikura desu ka?* |
| Is breakfast included? | 朝食付ですか？ | *Chō shoku tsuki desu ka?* |
| Do you have a reduction for children? | 子供料金はありま すか？ | *Kodomo ryōkin wa arimasu ka?* |
| Is there… | …はありますか | *... wa arimasu ka?* |
| - a swimming pool? | スイミングプールはあ りますか？ | *Suimingu pūru wa arimasu ka?* |
| - a lift? | エレベータはありま すか？ | *Erebēta wa arimasu ka?* |

| I'll take it | それにします | *Sore ni shimasu* |
| Can I pay by... | 支払は、…でよいですか? | *Shiharai wa ... de yoi desu ka?* |
| - credit card? | …クレジットカード | *... kurejitto kādo ...* |
| - traveller's cheque? | …トラベラーズチェック | *... toraberāzu chekku ...* |

## Special requests

| Could you... | … てもらえますか? | *... te moraemasu ka?* |
| | …でください | *... te/de kudasai* |
| - put this in the hotel safe? | ホテルの金庫に入れてもらえますか? | *Hoteru no kinko ni irete moraemasu ka?* |
| - order a taxi for me? | タクシーを呼んでください | *Takushī o yonde kudasai* |
| - wake me up at (7am) | (7時) に起してください | *(shichi ji) ni okoshite kudasai* |
| Can I have... | …にできますか? | *... ni dekimasu ka?* |
| - a room with a sea view? | 海が見える部屋にできますか? | *Umi ga mieru heya ni dekimasu ka?* |
| - a bigger room? | 大きな部屋にできますか? | *Ōkina heya ni dekimasu ka?* |
| - a quieter room? | 静かな部屋にできますか? | *Shizukana heya ni dekimasu ka?* |

## Business hotels

Handily located around all major stations, business hotels are an option you should consider as they offer basic but comfortable accommodation at reasonable prices.

| Is there... | …はありますか？ | ... wa arimasuka? |
| - a safe? | 金庫… | Kinko ... |
| - a babysitting service? | 託児所… | Takujijo shisetsu ... |
| - a laundry service? | ランドリーサービス… | Randorī sābisu ... |
| | | |
| Is there wheelchair access? | 車イスで行けますか？ | Kuruma isu de ikemasu ka? |
| I have a reservation for tonight in the name of... | …の名前で、予約をとっているのですが | ... no namae de, yoyaku o totte iru no desu ga |

## Checking in & out

| Here's my passport | 私のパスポートです | Watashi no pasupōto desu |
| What time is check out? | チェックアウトは何時ですか | Chekku auto wa nanji desu ka? |
| Can I have a later check out? | チェックアウトを遅くできますか？ | Chekku auto o osoku dekimasu ka? |
| Can I leave my bags here? | 荷物を置いていても良いですか？ | Nimotsu o oite itemo yoi desu ka? |
| I'd like to check out | チェックアウトをしたいのですが | Chekku auto o sitai no desu ga |
| Can I have the bill? | 支払をできますか？ | Shiharai o dekimasu ka? |

## Price or place

When you are selecting a hotel, consider the location as well as the price – you don't want to bankrupt yourself travelling! Hotels located near major sites such as the Kyoto Tower apply a hefty convenience mark-up. When selecting a hotel, consider the location as well as the price – you don't want to bankrupt yourself travelling!

# Survival Guide

Survival is not a problem in this most modern of countries. Most public telephones in Japan are green and take cards ranging from 500 to 10,000 yen (some also take coins). Post offices are indicated by a capital T with a bar over it (〒), and are usually open from 9am to 5pm, although main post offices are open 24 hours. Banks are open from 9am to 3pm, with ATMs usually accessible until 9pm. Convenience stores also have ATMs from which cash can be withdrawn 24 hours a day. Chemists are usually open from 9am to 9pm, but some drugstores stay open until midnight. Medical treatment is expensive, so travel insurance is essential.

## Money & banks

| | | |
|---|---|---|
| Where is the nearest… | この近くに…ありますか？ | *Kono chikaku ni ... arimasu ka?* |
| - bank? | - 銀行 | - *ginkō* |
| - ATM? | - ATM | - *ATM* |
| - bureau de change? | - 両替所 | - *ryōgaejo* |
| | | |
| I'd like to… | …したいんですが | *...shitain desu ga* |
| - withdraw money | お金をおろ… | *Okane o oro ...* |
| - cash a traveller's cheque | トラベラーズチェックを換金… | *Toraberāzu chekku o kankin ...* |
| - change money | (currency)を換え… | *(currency) o ryogae ...* |
| - arrange a transfer | 送金する… | *Soukin ...* |
| | | |
| Could I have smaller notes, please? | 小額紙幣でお願いできますか？ | *Shogakushihei de onegaidekimasuka?* |
| What's the exchange rate? | 為替レートはいくらですか？ | *Kawase rēto wa ikura desu ka?* |
| What's the commission? | 手数料はいくらですか？ | *Tesuuryou wa ikura desu ka?* |
| | | |
| What's the charge for... | ～の手数料はいくらですか？ | *... no tesuuryou wa ikura desu ka?* |
| - making a withdrawal | 預金を引き出す… | *Yokin o hikidasu ...* |
| - exchanging money | 両替をする… | *Ryōgae o suru ...* |
| - cashing a cheque? | 小切手を換金する… | *Kogitte o kankin suru ...* |

お手洗い

**TOILET**

←

### In conveniences
Public toilets can be challenging: you have to squat and toilet paper may be lacking. Fortunately, department stores respect squatters' rights: their toilets are both clean and well stocked.

| What's the minimum/ maximum amount? | 最低金額/最高金額は いくらですか？ | *Saitei kingaku/ saikō kingaku wa ikura desu ka?* |
| This is not right | これでは合ってい ません | *Koredewa atteimasen* |
| Is there a problem with my account? | 私の口座に問題があり ますか？ | *Watashino kōza ni mondai ga arimasuka?* |
| The ATM took my card | ATMからカードが出 てきません | *ATM kara kādo ga detekimasen* |
| I've forgotten my PIN | 暗証番号を忘れました | *Anshō bangō o wasuremashita* |

## Post office

| Where is the (main) post office? | 郵便局はどこですか？ | *Yūbinkyoku wa doko desu ka?* |
| I'd like to send a… | …を送りたいんで すが | *... o okuritain desu ga* |
| - letter | 手紙… | *Tegami ...* |
| - postcard | 葉書… | *Hagaki ...* |
| - parcel | 小包… | *Kozutsumi ...* |
| - fax | ファックス… | *Fakkusu ...* |
| I'd like to send this... | これを….送りたいの ですが | *Kore o ... okuritaino desu ga* |
| - to the United Kingdom | イギリスに | *- Igirisu ni* |
| - by airmail | 航空便で | *- kōkūbin de* |
| - by express mail | 速達で | *- sokutatsu de* |
| - by registered mail | 書留で | *- kakitome de* |
| I'd like | …をください | *... o kudasai* |
| - a stamp for this letter/postcard | この手紙/葉書の 切手 … | *Kono tegami/ hagaki no kitte ...* |
| I'd like to buy envelopes | 封筒を買いたいの ですが | *Futō o kaitaino desu ga* |
| I'd like to make a photocopy | コピーしたいんですが | *Kopī o shitain desu ga* |

## Telecoms

| Where can I make an international phone call? | 国際電話は、どこでで きますか？ | *Kokusai denwa wa, doko de dekimasu ka?* |

| Where can I buy a phone card? | テレホンカードは、どこで買えますか？ | *Terehon kādo wa, doko de kaemasu ka?* |
| How do I call abroad? | 国際電話はどうやってかけますか？ | *Kokusai denwa wa douyatte kakemasu ka?* |
| How much does it cost per minute? | 一分いくらですか？ | *Ippunn ikura desu ka?* |
| The number is... | 番号は… | *Bangō wa ...* |
| What's the area/ country code for...? | 局番/国番号は何番ですか？ | *Kyokuban/kuni bangō wa nanban desu ka?* |
| The number is engaged | 話中です | *Hanashichū desu* |
| The connection is bad | 接続が悪いです | *Setsuzoku ga warui desu* |
| I've been cut off | 電話が切れました | *Denwa ga kiremashita* |
| I'd like... | …が欲しいのですですが | *... ga hoshiino desu ga* |
| - a charger for my mobile phone | 携帯用充電器 | *Keitaiyō jūdenki* |
| - an adaptor plug | アダプタープラグ | *Adaputaa puragu* |
| - a pre-paid SIM card | プリペイドSIMカード | *Puripeido SIM kādo* |

## Making international calls

You can make international calls from any public phone with the sign INTERNATIONAL AND DOMESTIC CARD/COIN TELEPHONE. Three companies provide international phone services: KKDI (001 44), ISD (0041 44) and IDC (0061 44).

## Internet

| Where's the nearest Internet café? | 一番近いインターネットカフェはどこですか？ | *Ichiban chikai intānetto kafe wa doko desu ka?* |
| Can I access the | ここでインターネッ | *Kokode intānetto* |

| Internet here? | トにアクセスできますか？ | ni akusesu dekimasuka? |
| How much is it... | … いくらですか？ | ... wa ikura desu ka? |
| - per minute? | 一分… | Ippun ... |
| - per hour? | 一時間… | Ichi ji kan ... |
| - to buy a CD? | CD… | Shī Dī ... |
| How do I... | どうやって….しますか？ | Douyatte ...shimasuka? |
| - log on? | どうやってログインしますか？ | Douyatte roguin shimasuka? |
| - open a browser? | どうやってブラウザーを開きますか？ | Douyatte burauzā o hirakimasuka? |
| - print this? | どうやってこれをプリントしますか？ | Dou yatte kore wo purinto shimasuka? |
| I need help with this computer | このコンピューターのことで助けてください | Kono konpuutā nokotode tasukete kudasai |
| The computer has crashed | コンピューターがクラッシュしました | Konpuutā ga kurasshu shimashita |
| I've finished | 終わりました | Owarimashita |

## Chemist

| Where's the nearest (all-night) chemist? | (夜間営業の）薬局はどこですか？ | (Yakan eigyō no) yakkyoku wa doko desu ka? |
| What time does the chemist open/close? | 薬局は何時に開きます/閉まりますか？ | Yakkyoku wa nanji ni akimasu/shimarimasu ka? |
| I need medicine for ... | …に効くものが欲しいです | ... ni kikumono ga hoshiidesu |
| - diarrhoea | 下痢… | Geri ... |
| - a cold | 風邪… | Kaze ... |
| - a cough | 咳… | Seki ... |
| - insect bites | 虫刺され… | Mushi sasare ... |
| - sunburn | 日焼け… | Hiyake ... |
| - motion sickness | 乗物酔い… | Norimo no yoi ... |
| - hay fever | 花粉症… | Kafunshō ... |
| I'd like... | …が欲しいんですが… | ...ga hoshiin desu ga ... |
| - aspirin | アスピリン… | Asupirin ... |

| | | |
|---|---|---|
| - plasters | 絆創膏… | *Bansōkō ...* |
| - condoms | コンドーム… | *Kondōmu ...* |
| - insect repellent | 虫除け… | *Mushiyoke ...* |
| - painkillers | 痛み止め… | *Itamidome ...* |
| - a (oral) contraceptive | 経口避妊薬… | *Keikō hinin yaku ...* |
| | | |
| How much should I take? | どのぐらい服用したらいいですか？ | *Donokurai fukuyou shitaraii desu ka?* |
| Take... | …服用してください | *... fukuyou shitekudsai* |
| | | |
| - a tablet | 1錠… | *Ichi jou ...* |
| - a teaspoon | 1匙… | *Hito saji ...* |
| - with water | 水で… | *Mizu de ...* |
| How often should I take this? | どれぐらいの頻度で服用しますか？ | *Dorekuraino hindo de fukuyou shimasuka?* |
| | | |
| - once/twice a day | 一日一回/二回 | *Ichi nichi ikkai/nikai* |
| - before/after meals | 食前/食後 | *Shokuzen/shokugo* |
| - in the morning/ evening | 朝/夕方 | *Asa/yūgata* |
| | | |
| Is it suitable for children? | 子供でも飲めますか？ | *Kodomo demo nomemasu ka?* |
| Will it make me drowsy? | 眠気を催すことがありますか？ | *Nemuke o moyoosu koto ga arimasu ka?* |
| | | |
| Do I need a prescription? | 処方箋が必要ですか？ | *Shohousen ga hituyou desu ka?* |
| I have a prescription | 処方箋を持ってます | *Shohousen o mottemasu* |

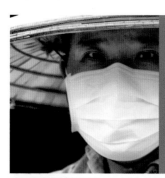

## Allergies

People with allergies have to be careful in Japan. MSG is used everywhere and cedar pollen causes severe hay fever. Most people take antihistamines and wear masks for protection.

# Children

| Where is the nearest… | この近くに…ありますか？ | Kono chikaku ni ... arimasu ka? |
|---|---|---|
| - playground? | - 運動場 | - undōjō |
| - fairground? | - 遊園地 | - yūenchi |
| - zoo? | - 動物園 | - dōbutsuen |
| - park? | - 公園 | - kōen |
| - swimming pool? | - プール | - pūru |

| Is this suitable for children? | 子供でも大丈夫ですか？ | Kodomo demo daijōbu desu ka? |
|---|---|---|
| Are children allowed? | 子供は大丈夫ですか？ | Kodomo wa daijoubu desu ka? |
| Are there baby-changing facilities here? | ベビールームはここにありますか？ | Bebii rūmu wa kokoni arimasu ka? |

| Do you have… | …ありますか？ | ... arimasu ka? |
|---|---|---|
| - a children's menu? | - 子供のメニューは… | Kodomo no menyū wa ... |
| - a high chair? | - ハイチェアー | Haicheā ... |

| Is there… | …はありますか？ | …wa arimasu ka? |
|---|---|---|
| - a child-minding service? | 保育サービスはありますか？ | Hoiku saabisu ... |
| - a nursery | 託児室 | Takujishitsu ... |

| Are the children constantly supervised? | 子供たちは常に見て貰えますか？ | Kodomotachi wa tsuneni mite moraemasu ka? |
|---|---|---|
| When can I bring them? | いつ引き取りにくればよいですか？ | Itsu hikitori ni kureba yoi desu ka? |
| What time do I have to pick them up? | 何時に引き取りにこなければいけませんか？ | Nanji ni hikitorini konakereba ikemasen ka? |
| He/she is ... years old | …は…歳です | ... wa ... sai desu |

| I'd like to buy… | …を買いたいです | ... o kaitai |
|---|---|---|
| - nappies | おむつ… | Omutsu ... |
| - baby wipes | お尻拭き… | Oshiri fuki ... |
| - tissues | ティシュパーパー… | Tisshu pēpā ... |

## Access all areas

Japan is getting easier for travellers in wheelchairs, but it is still far from ideal. The underground can be especially difficult to negotiate, though station staff will help you to get on the train.

## Travellers with disabilities

| | | |
|---|---|---|
| I have a disability | 体が不自由です | Karada ga fujiyū desu |
| I need assistance | 手伝ってください | Tetsudatte kudasai |
| I am blind | 私は目が見えません | Watashi wa me ga miemasen |
| I am deaf | 私は耳が聞こえません | Watashi wa mimi ga kikoemasen |
| I have a hearing aid | 私は補聴器をつけています | Watashi wa hochōki o tsuketeimasu |
| I can't walk well | 歩くのが不自由です | Aruku noga fujiyuu desu |
| Is there a lift? | エレベーターがありますか? | Erebētā ga arimasu ka? |
| Is there wheelchair access? | 車椅子用入り口はありますか? | Kuruma isu yō iriguchi wa arimasu ka? |
| Can I bring my guide dog? | 盲導犬を連れて入れますか? | Mōdōken o tsurete hairemasuka? |
| Are there disabled toilets? | 障害者用トイレはありますか? | Shōgaisha yō toire wa arimasuka? |
| Do you offer disabled services? | 障害者サービスを希望しますか? | Shōgaisha saabisu o kibō shimasuka? |
| Could you help me... | …のを手伝っていただけますか? | ... no o tetsudatte itadakemasuka? |
| - cross the street | 道路を渡 …る | Dōro o wataru ... |
| - go up/down the stairs? | 階段を上る/下りる… | Kaidan o noboru/oriru ... |
| Can I sit down somewhere? | どこかに座れますか? | Dokokani suwaremasuka? |

| Could you call an accessible taxi for me? | 障害者用タクシーを呼んでもらえますか？ | *Shōgaishayō takusii o yondemora-emasuka?* |

## Repairs & cleaning

| This is broken | これは壊れています | *Kore wa kowarete imasu* |
| Can you fix it? | 修理できますか | *Shuri dekimasu ka?* |
| Do you have... | …がありますか？ | *... ga arimasu ka?* |
| - a battery? | 電池 … | *Denchi ...* |
| - spare parts? | 予備部品 … | *Yobi buhin ...* |
| Can you ... this? | これを…ことができますか | *Kore o ... koto ga dekimasu ka?* |
| - clean | - きれいにする | *- kirei ni suru* |
| - press | - アイロン | *- airon o kakeru* |
| - dry-clean | - をドライクリーニングする | *- dorai kurīnigu suru* |
| - patch | - つぎ当てする | *- tsugiate suru* |
| When will it be ready? | いつできますか？ | *Itsu dekimasu ka?* |

## Tourist information

| Where's the Tourist Information Office? | 観光案内所はどこけすか？ | *Kankō annaijo wa doko desu ka?* |
| Do you have a city map? | 都市地図がありますか？ | *Toshi chizu ga arimasu ka?* |
| What are the main places of interest? | 観光名所はどこですか？ | *Kankō meisho wa doko desu ka?* |
| Could you show me on the map? | 地図で見せてくれませんか？ | *Chizu de misete kuremasen ka?* |
| We'll be here for... | …ここにいます | *... koko ni imasu* |
| - half a day | 半日… | *Han nichi ...* |
| - a day | 1日 … | *Ichi nichi ...* |
| - a week | 一週間 … | *Isshū kan ...* |

## Finding the way home
If you get lost, you need two things: this guide and a brochure from your hotel. Just speak and point.

| Do you have a brochure in English? | 英語のパンフレットがありますか | *Eigo no panfuretto ga arimasu ka?* |
| We're interested in... | 私たちは…に興味があります | *Watashitachi wa ... ni kyōmi ga arimasu* |
| - history/ architecture | - 歴史/建築学 | - *rekisi/ kenchikugaku* |
| - shopping | - ショッピング | - *shoppingu* |
| - hiking | - ハイキング | - *haikingu* |
| - a scenic walk | - 景色を見ながらの散歩 | - *keshiki o minagara no sanpo* |
| - a boat cruise | - ボートクルーズ | - *bōto kurūzu* |
| - a guided tour | - ガイド付きツアー | - *gaido tsuki tsuā* |
| Are there any excursions? | 遊覧旅行がありますか？ | *Yūran ryokō ga arimasu ka?* |
| How long does it take? | どのくらいかかりますか？ | *Dono kurai kakarimasu ka?* |
| What does it cost? | いくらかかりますか？ | *Ikura kakarimasu ka?* |
| What days is it open/closed? | 何曜日開いて/閉まっていますか？ | *Naniyoubi aite/ shimatte imasu ka?* |
| What time does it open/close? | 開館/閉館は何時ですか？ | *Kaikan/heikan wa nanji desu ka?* |
| What's the admission price? | 入場料はいくらですか？ | *Nyūjōryō wa ikura desu ka?* |
| Are there any tours in English? | 英語のツアーがありますか？ | *Eigo no tsuā ga arimasu ka?* |

## Police protocol

If you are stopped by the police for any reason, do not respond with anger and indignation: this will only exacerbate the problem. A smile and an apology if and when necessary is always the best response.

非常口
EXIT

# Emergencies

If you need urgent help, call the Japan
Helpline (0570-000-911) for English-
language assistance. The police operate
an English-speaking service and there
are hospitals with staff that speak
English, although they all keep normal
working hours. If you get through to
an operator who only speaks Japanese,
do not panic. Speak clearly and slowly
(using the expressions in this language
guide). The police can be difficult to
handle, but if you keep calm and adopt
an apologetic attitude, they are generally
lenient. If you lose anything, always
report it to the police: there is a good
chance it will be returned.

# Medical

| Where is... | … どこですか？ | ... doko desu ka? |
|---|---|---|
| - the hospital? | 病院はどこですか？ | Byōin wa doko desu ka? |
| - the health centre? | 医療センターはどこで すか？ | Iryō sentā wa doko desu ka? |
| | | |
| Is there... | … いますか？ | ... imasu ka? |
| - a doctor? | 医者はいますか？ | Isha wa imasu ka? |
| - a female doctor? | 女性の医者はいま すか？ | Josē no isha wa imasu ka? |
| Please call an ambulance | 救急車を呼んでく ださい | Kyūkyūsha o yonde kudasai |
| It's very urgent | 大至急です | Daishikyū desu |
| I'm injured | けがをしました | Kega o shimashita |
| Can I see a doctor? | 医者にみてもらえ ますか | Isha ni mite moraemasu ka? |
| I don't feel well | 気分が良くないです | Kibun ga yokunai desu |
| I have a cold | 風邪をひいています | Kaze o hiite imasu |
| I have diarrhoea | 下痢をしています | Geri o shite imasu |
| I have a rash | 発疹があります | Hasshin ga arimasu |
| I have a temperature | 熱があります | Netsu ga arimasu |
| I have a lump here | ここにしこりがあ ります | Koko ni shikori ga arimasu |
| It hurts here | ここが痛いです | Koko ga itai desu |
| It hurts a lot/a little | とても/少し痛い | Totemo/sukoshi itai desu |
| How much do I owe you? | いくらですか？ | Ikura desu ka? |
| I have insurance | 保険があります | Hoken ga arimasu |

## Calling for help

The following telephone numbers are useful in emergencies: Japan Helpline: 0570-000-911; Police: 110; Ambulance: 119

# Dentist

| | | |
|---|---|---|
| I need a dentist | 歯医者さんがいますか？ | *Haisha-san ga imasu ka?* |
| I have tooth ache | 歯が痛いです | *Ha ga itai desu* |
| My gums are swollen | 歯ぐきがはれています | *Haguki ga harete imasu* |
| This filling has fallen out | 詰め物がとれました | *Tsumemono ga toremashita* |
| I have an abscess | 歯がはれています | *Ha ga harete imasu* |
| I have broken a tooth | 歯が折れました | *Ha ga oremashita* |
| Are you going to take it out? | 歯を抜きますか？ | *Ha o nukimasu ka?* |
| Can you fix it temporarily? | 仮の治療ができますか？ | *Kari no chiryō ga dekimasu ka?* |

# Crime

| | | |
|---|---|---|
| I want to report a theft | 被害届けを出したいんですが | *Higai todoke o dashitain desu ga* |
| Someone has stolen my... | …盗まれました | *...nusumare mashita* |
| - bag | かばんを盗まれました | *Kaban o nusumare mashita* |
| - car | 車を盗まれました | *Kuruma o nusumare mashita* |
| - credit cards | クレジットカードを盗まれました | *Kurejitto kādo o nusumare mashita* |
| - money | お金を盗まれました | *Okane o nusumare mashita* |
| - passport | パスポートを盗まれました | *Pasupōto o nusumare mashita* |

# Lost property

| | | |
|---|---|---|
| I've been attacked | 泥棒に襲われました | *Dorobō ni osowaremashita* |
| I've lost my... | … をなくしました | *...wo nakushimashita* |
| - car keys | 車の鍵 … | *Kuruma no kagi ...* |
| - driving licence | 運転免許証 … | *Unten menkyoshō ...* |
| - handbag | ハンドバッグ … | *Handobaggu ...* |
| - flight tickets | 飛行機の切符 … | *Hikōki no kippu ...* |
| It happened... | … 起きました | *... okimashita* |
| - this morning | けさ… | *Kesa ...* |

| - today | 今日 … | *Kyō …* |
| - in the hotel | ホテルで … | *Hoteru de …* |
| I left it in the taxi | タクシーに忘れました | *Takushī ni wasuremashita* |

## Breakdown

| I've had... | | |
| - an accident | 事故に遭いました | *Jiko ni aimashita* |
| - a breakdown | 車が故障しました | *Kuruma ga koshō shimashita* |
| - a puncture | パンクしました | *Panku shimashita* |
| My battery is flat | バッテリーがなくなりました | *Batterī ga nakunarimashita* |
| I don't have a spare tyre | スペアタイヤがありません | *Supea taiya ga arimasen* |
| I've run out of petrol | ガソリンがありません | *Gasorin ga arimasen* |
| My car won't start | エンジンがかかりません | *Enjin ga kakarimasen* |
| Can you repair it? | 修理してもらえますか？ | *Shūri shite moraemasu ka?* |
| How long will it take? | どのぐらいかかりますか？ | *Donogurai kakarimasu ka?* |
| I have breakdown cover | 車の保険があります | *Kuruma no hoken ga arimasu* |

## Problems with the authorities

| I'm sorry, I didn't realise... | すみません…気がつきませんでした | *Sumimasen, ... ki ga tsukimasen deshita* |
| - I was driving so fast | -スピード違反に… | - *supīdo ihan ni ...* |
| - I went over the red lights | - 信号無視に… | - *shingō mushi ni ...* |
| - it was against the law | - 違反だと知りませんでした | - *ihan da to shirimasen deshita* |
| Here is my passport | 私のパスポートです | *Watashi no pasupōto desu* |
| I'm innocent | 無実です | *Mujitsu desu* |

# Dictionary

This section has two parts: an
English-Japanese dictionary to
help you get your point across and
a Japanese-English one to help you
decipher the reply. Characters that
you are likely to see on signs are
highlighted in magenta in the
Japanese-English section (pp80–94).
Where there's possible ambiguity,
a guide word is given in brackets.
There are two forms of all Japanese
verbs – the plain and the polite. Both
are given here, with the plain form
in brackets. You should use only the
polite form. Long vowels are indicated
by a macron. For example, *hikōki* is
pronounced *hi koo ki*.

# English-Japanese dictionary

## A

| about (concerning) | について | Ni tsuite |
| accident (traffic) | 交通事故 | Kōtsū jiko |
| accommodation | 宿泊設備 | Shukuhaku setsubi |
| aeroplane | 飛行機 | Hikōki |
| again | もう一度 | Mō ichi do |
| ... ago | … 前 | ... mae |
| AIDS | エイズ | Ēizu |
| airmail | 航空便 | Kōkūbin |
| airport | 空港 | Kūkō |
| alarm (clock) | 目覚まし時計 | Mezamashi dokei |
| all | 皆 | Minna no |
| all right | 大丈夫 | Daijōbu |
| allergy | アレルギー | Arerugī |
| ambulance | 救急車 | Kyūkyūsha |
| America | アメリカ | Amerika |
| American ...(car, food, etc.) | アメリカの … | Amerika no ... |
| American (person) | アメリカ人 | Amerika jin |
| and | … と …, … や …, … に …, … も …, および | ... to ..., ... ya ..., ... ni ..., ... mo ..., oyobi |
| anniversary | 記念日 | Kinnenbi |
| another | ほかの/別の | Hokano/betsuno |
| to answer | 答える | Kotaeru |
| apartment | アパート/マンション | Apāto/manshon |
| appointment | 予約 | Yoyaku |
| April | 四月 | Shi gatsu |
| area | 地方 | Chihō |
| area code | 市外局番 | Shigai kyokuban |
| around (six o' clock) | （六時）ごろ | (Rokuji) goro |
| to arrange | （準備する）します | (Junbi suru) shimasu |
| arrival | 到着 | Tōchaku |
| art | 芸術 | Geijutsu |
| to ask (inquire) | 尋ねる | Tazuneru |
| aspirin | アスピリン | Asupirin |
| at (time) | … に | ... ni |
| August | 八月 | Hachi gatsu |
| Australia | オーストラリア | Ōsutoraria |
| Australian | オーストラリア人 | Ōsutoraria jin |
| away | 離れて | Hanarete |

## B

| baby | 赤ちゃん | Akachan |
| back (body) | 背中 | Senaka |
| back (place) | 後ろ | Ushiro |
| bad | 悪い | Warui |
| baggage | 荷物 | Nimotsu |

| bar (pub) | バー | *Bā* |

| **bath** | お風呂 | *Ofuro* |

The Japanese never use soap or shampoo in the bath, which is solely for relaxing in.

| to be (for living things) | (居る) います | *(Iru) imasu* |
| to be (for inanimate objects) | (ある) あります | *(Aru) arimasu* |
| beach | 海岸／ビーチ | *Kaigan/bīchi* |
| because ... | … から | *... kara* |
| because of ... | … のために… | *... no tame ni* |
| best | 一番いい | *Ichiban ii* |
| better | もっといい | *Motto ii* |
| between | の間 | *No aida* |
| bicycle | 自転車 | *Jitensha* |
| big | 大きい | *Ōki* |
| bill | 勘定 | *Kanjō* |
| bit (a) | 少し | *Sukoshi* |
| boarding card | 搭乗券 | *Tōjōken* |
| book | 本 | *Hon* |
| to book | 予約（する）します | *Yoyaku (suru) shimasu* |
| booking | 予約 | *Yoyaku* |
| box office | 切符売場 | *Kippu uriba* |
| boy | 男の子 | *Otoko no ko* |
| brother (one's elder) | 兄 | *Ani* |
| brother (one's younger) | 弟 | *Otōto* |
| bureau de change | 両替店 | *Ryōgae ten* |
| to burn | (焼く) 焼きます | *(Yaku) yakimasu* |
| bus | バス | *Basu* |
| business | 仕事 | *Shigoto* |
| business card | 名刺 | *Meishi* |
| but | しかし | *Shikashi* |
| to buy | (買う) 買います | *(Kau) kaimasu* |
| by (air, car, etc) | (飛行機、車、など) で | *(Hikōki, kuruma, nado) de* |
| by (beside) | … のそばに | *... no soba ni* |
| by (via) | … で | *... de* |

C

| café | 喫茶店 | *Kissaten* |
| to call | 電話（する）します | *Denwa (suru) shimasu* |
| camera | カメラ | *Kamera* |
| can (to be able) | (できる) できます | *(Dekiru) dekimasu* |
| to cancel | キャンセル（する）します | *Kyanseru (suru) shimasu* |
| car | 車 | *Kuruma* |

| carnival | カーニバル | *kānibaru* |
| cash | 現金 | *Genkin* |
| to cash | 換金（する）します | *Kankin (suru) shimasu* |
| cash point | キャッシュコーナー | *Kyasshu kōnā* |
| casino | カジノ | *Kajino* |
| castle | お城 | *Oshiro* |
| cathedral | 大聖堂 | *Daiseidō* |
| CD | CD | *Shī Dī* |
| centre | 中心 | *Chūshin* |
| to change (one's clothes) | 着替える | *(Kigaeru) kigaemasu* |
| to change (trains, etc.) | （乗り換える）乗り換えます | *(Norikaeru) norikaemasu* |
| to change (money) | 両替する（します） | *Ryōgae (suru) shimasu* |
| charge | 料金 | *Ryōkin* |
| to charge (credit card) | カードで（はらう）払います | *Kādo de (harau) haraimasu* |
| cheap | 安い | *Yasui* |
| to check in | チェックイン（する）します | *Chekku in (suru) shimasu* |

| **cheers (toast)** | 乾杯 | ***Kanpai*** |
| --- | --- | --- |

**Use the word *kanpai* when proposing a toast. Never say "chin chin" – it's slang for "penis".**

| cheque | チェック | *Chekku* |
| cherry blossoms | 桜 | *Sakura* |
| cherry blossom viewing | 花見 | *Hanami* |
| child | 子供 | *Kodomo* |
| to choose | 選ぶ | *Erabu* |
| cigar | 葉巻 | *Hamaki* |
| cigarette | タバコ | *Tabako* |
| cinema | 映画館 | *Eigakan* |
| city | 都市 | *Toshi* |
| to close | （閉める）閉めます | *(Shimeru) shimemasu* |
| close by | 近い | *Chikai* |
| closed | 閉館 | *Heikan* |
| clothes | 服 | *Fuku* |
| clothes (Western) | 洋服 | *Yōfuku* |
| club | クラブ | *Kurabu* |
| coast | 海岸 | *Kaigan* |
| coffee house | 喫茶店 | *Kissaten* |
| cold (weather) | 寒い | *Samui* |
| colour | 色 | *Iro* |
| to complain | 文句を（言う）いいます | *Monku o (iu) iimasu* |
| complaint | 文句 | *Monku* |
| computer | コンピュータ | *Konpyūta* |

| to confirm | 確認（する）します | *Kakunin (suru) shimasu* |
| confirmation | 確証 | *Kakushō* |
| consulate | 領事館 | *Ryōjikan* |
| to contact | 連絡（する）します | *Renraku (suru) shimasu* |
| contagious | 伝染性 | *Densensei* |
| cool | 涼しい | *Suzushī* |
| cost | 費用 | *Hiyō* |
| to cost | かかります | *Kakarimasu* |
| cot | 折りたたみ式ベッド | *Oritatami shiki beddo* |
| country | 国 | *Kuni* |
| countryside | 田舎 | *Inaka* |
| cream | クリーム | *Kurīmu* |
| credit card | クレジットカード | *Kurejitto kādo* |
| crime | 犯罪 | *Hanzai* |
| currency | 通貨 | *Tsūka* |
| customer | お客さん | *Okyaku san* |
| customs | 税関 | *Zeikan* |
| cut (wound) | 傷 | *Kizu* |
| to cut | カット（する）します | *Katto (suru) shimasu* |
| cycling | サイクリング | *Saikuringu* |

D

| damage | 被害 | *Higai* |
| to damage | （壊す）壊します | *(Kowasu) kowashimasu* |
| danger | 危険 | *Kiken* |
| daughter | 娘 | *Musume* |
| day | 日 | *Hi* |
| December | 十二月 | *Jūni gatsu* |
| to dehydrate | 脱水（する）します | *Dassui (suru) shimasu* |
| delay | （遅れる）遅れます | *(Okureru) okuremasu* |
| to dial | 電話を（かける）かけます | *Denwa o (kakeru) kakemasu* |
| difficult | 難しい | *Muzukashii* |
| directions | 方向 | *Hōkō* |
| dirty | 汚い | *Kitanai* |
| disabled | 身体障害者 | *Shintai shōgai sha* |
| discount | 割引 | *Waribiki* |
| district | 地区 | *Chiku* |

| **to disturb** | おじゃまします | ***Ojama shimasu*** |

When visiting someone, the Japanese will greet that person with *ojama shimasu* ("Excuse me, I am going to disturb you").

| doctor | 医者 | *Isha* |
| doll | 人形 | *Ningyō* |

| double | ダブル | *Daburu* |
| down | 下 | *Shita* |
| to drive | 運転（する）します | *Unten (suru) shimasu* |
| driver | 運転手 | *Untenshu* |
| driving licence | 運転免許証 | *Unten menkyoshō* |
| drug | 麻薬 | *Mayaku* |
| drunk | 酔っぱらった | *Yopparatta* |
| to dry clean | ドライクリーニング（する）します | *Doraikurīnigu (suru) shimasu* |
| dry cleaner's | ドライクリーニング店 | *Doraikurīningu ten* |
| during | の間 | *No aida* |
| duty (tax) | 関税 | *Kanzei* |

E

| early | 早い | *Hayai* |
| e-mail | 電子メール | *Denshi mēru* |
| embassy | 大使館 | *Taishikan* |
| emergency | 緊急 | *kinkyū* |
| England | イギリス | *Igirisu* |
| English | 英語 | *Eigo* |
| enough | 十分 | *Jūbun* |
| entrance | 入口 | *Iriguchi* |
| error | 間違い | *Machigai* |
| exactly | ちょうど | *Chōdo* |
| exchange rate | 為替レート | *Kawase rēto* |
| exhibition | 展覧会 | *tenrankai* |
| exit | 出口 | *Deguchi* |
| express (delivery) | 速達 | *Sokutatsu* |
| express (train) | 急行 | *Kyūkō* |

F

| facilities | 設備 | *Setsubi* |
| far | 遠い | *Tooi* |
| father | お父さん | *Otō-san* |
| favourite | いちばん好きな … | *Ichi ban sukina ...* |
| February | 二月 | *Ni gatsu* |

| **festival** | 祭 | ***Matsuri*** |

There are dozens of boisterous festivals in Japan, especially in the summer and autumn.

| film (camera) | フィルム | *Firumu* |
| film (cinema) | 映画 | *Eiga* |
| fire | 火事 | *Kaji* |
| fire exit | 非常口 | *Hijō guchi* |
| first aid | 応急手当 | *Okyūteate* |
| fitting room | 試着室 | *Shickaku shitsu* |
| flight | 便 | *Bin* |
| flu | インフルエンザ | *Infuruenza* |
| food poisoning | 食中毒 | *Shoku chūdoku* |
| football | サッカー | *Sakkā* |

| | | |
|---|---|---|
| for ... (in order to) | … のために | ... no tame ni |
| foreigner | 外国人/外人 | Gaikoku jin/gaijin |
| form (document) | 用紙 | Yōshi |
| four | 四 | Shi/yon |
| free | 自由 | Jiyū |
| free (money) | 無料 | Muryō |
| friend | 友達 | Tomodachi |
| from | から | Kara |

| **front door** | **玄関** | ***Genkan*** |
|---|---|---|

The *genkan* is actually a small foyer where people remove or put on their shoes.

### G

| | | |
|---|---|---|
| gallery | ギャラリー | Gyararī |
| garage | 修理工場/ガソリンスタンド | Shūrikōjō/gasorin sutando |
| gas | ガス | Gasu |
| gents (toilets) | 男性用トイレ | Dansei yo toire |
| girl | 女の子 | Onna no ko |
| glasses | めがね | Megane |
| golf | ゴルフ | Gorufu |
| golf course | ゴルフ場 | Gorufu jō |
| good | 良い/いい | Yoi/ii |
| group | グループ | Gurūpu |
| guarantee | 保証 | Hoshō |
| guide | ガイド | Gaido |

### H

| | | |
|---|---|---|
| hair | 髪 | Kami |
| hairdresser's | 美容院 | Biyouin |
| half | 半分 | Hanbun |
| heat | 熱 | Netsu |
| help! | 助けて！ | Tasukete! |
| here | ここ | Koko |
| high | 高い | Takai |
| holiday (work-free day) | 休日 | Kyūjitsu |
| holidays | 休暇 | Kyūka |
| homosexual | ホモセクシャル | Homosekushal |
| hospital | 病院 | Byōin |
| hot | 暑い | Atsui |
| hotel | ホテル | Hoteru |
| how? | どう/どれ/どの？ | Dō/dore/dono? |
| how big? | 大きさはどれぐらいですか？ | Ookisa wa dore gurai desu ka? |
| how far (how long does it take)? | どのぐらいかかりますか？ | Dono gurai kakarimasu ka? |
| how long (length)? | 長さはどれぐらいですか？ | Nagasa wa dore kurai desu ka? |
| how much? | いくらですか？ | Ikura desu ka? |

| | | |
|---|---|---|
| hurry up! | 急いで！ | *Isoide!* |
| husband (my/ someone else's) | 主人／ご主人 | *Shujin/goshujin* |

## I

| | | |
|---|---|---|
| identity card | 身分証明書 | *Mibun shōmeisyo* |
| ill | 病気 | *Byōki* |
| immediately | 直接 | *Chokusetsu* |
| important | 大切 | *Taisetsu* |
| in | の中に | *...no naka ni* |
| information | 情報 | *Jōhō* |
| inside | 中 | *Naka* |
| insurance | 保険 | *Hoken* |
| interesting | 面白い | *Omoshiroi* |
| international | 国際 | *Kokusai* |
| Internet | インターネット | *Intānetto* |
| Ireland | アイルランド | *Airurando* |
| Irish | アイルランド人 | *Airurando jin* |
| island | 島 | *Shima* |
| itinerary | 旅程 | *Ryotei* |

## J

| | | |
|---|---|---|
| January | 一月 | *Ichi gatsu* |
| jet ski | ジェット スキー | *Jetto sukī* |
| journey | 旅行 | *Ryokō* |
| July | 七月 | *Shichi gatsu* |
| junction | 交差点 | *Kōsaten* |
| June | 六月 | *Roku gatsu* |
| just (only) | …だけ | *... dake* |

## K

| | | |
|---|---|---|
| key | 鍵 | *Kagi* |
| key ring | キーホルダー | *Kī horudā* |
| keyboard | キーボード | *Kībōdo* |
| kid | 子供 | *Kodomo* |
| kind | 親切 | *Shinsetsu* |
| kind (person) | 優しい（人） | *Yasashii* |
| kind (sort) | 種類 | *Shurui* |
| kiosk | キオスク | *Kiosuku* |
| kiss | キス | *Kisu* |

## L

| | | |
|---|---|---|
| label | ラベル | *Raberu* |
| ladies (toilets) | 女性用トイレ | *Josei yo toire* |
| lady | 女のひと | *Onna no hito* |

| | | |
|---|---|---|
| **lake** | 湖／… 湖 | ***Mizuumi/... ko*** |

*Mizuumi* is the word for "lake". To refer to
a particular lake, use *ko* (e.g. Yamanaka-*ko*)

| language | 言語 | *Gengo* |
|---|---|---|
| last | 最後 | *Saigo* |
| late (delayed) | 遅れた | *Okureta* |
| late (time) | 遅い | *Osoi* |
| launderette | コインランドリー | *Koin randrī* |
| lawyer | 弁護士 | *Bengoshi* |
| less | 少ない | *Sukunai* |
| library | 図書館 | *Toshokan* |
| life jacket | 救命胴衣 | *Kyūmei dōi* |
| lifeguard | ライフガード | *Raifu gādo* |
| lift | エレベーター | *Erebētā* |
| like | 好きです | *Suki desu* |
| little | 小さい | *Chiisai* |
| local | 地元の | *Jimoto no* |
| to lose | (なくす) なくします | *(Nakusu) nakushimasu* |
| lost property | 忘れ物取扱所 | *Wasure mono toriatsukaijo* |
| luggage | 荷物 | *Nimotsu* |

## M

| madam | 奥様 | *Okusama* |
|---|---|---|
| mail | 郵便物 | *Yūbin butsu* |
| main | 主な | *Omona* |
| man | 男の人 | *Otoko no hito* |
| manager | 部長 | *Buchō* |
| many | たくさんの | *Takusan no* |
| map (city) | 地図 | *Chizu* |
| map (road) | 地図 | *Chizu* |
| March | 三月 | *San gatsu* |
| market | 市場 | *Ichiba* |
| married | 結婚して (いる) います | *Kekkon shite (iru) imasu* |

| **massage parlour** | ソープランド | *Sōpurando* |
|---|---|---|

**Although legally classed as massage parlours, "soaplands" are brothels. The word replaced "Turkish bath" after a protest by Turkey.**

| May | 五月 | *Go gatsu* |
|---|---|---|
| maybe | たぶん | *Tabun* |
| mechanic | 修理工 | *Shūrikō* |
| meeting | 会議 | *Kaigi* |
| message | 伝言 | *Dengon* |
| midday | 昼間 | *Hiruma* |
| midnight | 真夜中 | *Mayonaka* |
| minimum | 最低 | *Saitei* |
| minute | 分 | *Fun/pun* |
| missing | いなくなる | *Inakunaru* |
| mobile phone | 携帯電話 | *Keitai denwa* |
| moment | 瞬間 | *Shunkan* |

| money | お金 | Okane |
| more | もっと | Motto |
| mosquito | 蚊 | Ka |
| most | 一番（多く） | Ichi ban (ooku) |
| mother (my/ someone else's) | 母/お母さん | Haha/okāsan |
| much | たくさん | Takusan |
| museum | 博物館 | Hakubutsukan |
| musical (show) | ミュージカル | Myūjikaru |
| must | （…しなければなりません） | (…shinakereba narimasen) |
| | …しなければならない | …shinakereba naranai |
| my | 私の | Watashi no |

**N**

| name | 名前 | Namae |
| nationality | 国籍 | Kokuseki |
| near | 近い | Chikai |
| necessary | 必要 | Hitsuyō |
| never | 一度も …。ない | Ich do mo ... nai |
| new | 新しい | Atarashii |
| news | ニュース | Nyūsu |
| newspaper | 新聞 | Shimbun |
| next | 次 | Tsugi |
| next to | …のすぐそばに | ... no sugu soba ni |
| nice | すてきな | Sutekina |
| nice (people) | いい（人） | Ii (hito) |
| night | 夜 | Yoru |
| nightclub | ナイトクラブ | Naito kurabu |
| north | 北 | Kita |
| note (money) | お札 | Osatsu |
| nothing | なにも … ない | Nanimo ... nai |
| November | 十一月 | Jūichi gatsu |
| now | 今 | Ima |
| nowhere | どこも … ない | Dokomo ... nai |
| number (figure) | 数字 | Sūji |

**O**

| object | 物体 | Buttai |
| October | 十月 | Jūgatsu |
| off (switched) | 切れて（いる）います | Kirete (iru) imasu |
| office | オフィス/営業所 | Ofisu/eigyō sho |
| ok | 大丈夫 | Daijōbu |
| on... | … の上 | ... no ue |
| on (switched) | つけています | Tsukete imasu |
| once | 一度 | Ichi do |
| only | ただ | Tada |
| open | 開いて（いる）います | Aite (iru) imasu |
| to open | （開ける）開けます | (Akeru) akemasu |

| operator | オペレーター | *Operētā* |
| opposite (place) | 向かい | *Mukai* |
| optician's | 眼鏡屋 | *Megane ya* |
| or | … か … | *... ka ...* |
| other | 他の | *Hoka no* |
| out of order | 故障 | *koshō* |
| outdoor | 屋外 | *Okugai* |
| outside | 外 | *Soto* |
| overnight | 夜通し | *Yodooshi* |
| owner | 持ち主 | *Mochinushi* |
| oxygen | 酸素 | *Sanso* |

### P

| pachinko | パチンコ | *Pachinko* |
| painkiller | 鎮痛剤 | *Chintsū zai* |
| pair | ふたり | *Futari* |
| parents | 両親 | *Ryōshin* |
| park | 公園 | *Kōen* |
| parking | 駐車 | *Chūsha* |
| party | パーティー | *Pātī* |
| passport | パスポート | *Pasupōto* |
| people | 人々 | *Hito bito* |
| perhaps | たぶん | *Tabun* |
| person | 人 | *Hito* |
| petrol | ガソリン | *Gasorin* |
| petrol station | ガソリンスタンド | *Gasorin sutando* |
| photo | 写真 | *Shashin* |
| phrase book | 会話表現集 | *Kaiwahyōgen shū* |
| place | 場所 | *Basho* |
| platform | プラットホーム | *Purattohōmu* |
| police | 警察 | *Keisatsu* |
| police box | 交番 | *Kōban* |
| port (sea) | 港 | *Minato* |
| possible | 可能な | *Kanōna* |
| post | 郵便 | *Yūbin* |
| post office | 郵便局 | *Yūbinkyoku* |
| prescription | 処方箋 | *Shohōsen* |
| price | 値段 | *Nedan* |

---

**priority seat** 優先席 **_Yūsen seki_**
Every subway or train carriage has *yūsen seki*,
priority seats for elderly or disabled people or for
pregnant women.

---

| private | 個人的な | *Kojinteki na* |
| probably | たぶん | *Tabun* |
| problem | 問題 | *Mondai* |
| pub | パブ | *Pabu* |
| public transport | 公共交通機関 | *Kōkyō kōtsū kikan* |

## Q

| quality | 質 | *Shitsu* |
|---|---|---|
| quantity | 数量 | *Sūryō* |
| query | 質問 | *Shitsumon* |
| question | 質問 | *Shitsumon* |
| queue | … の列 | *... no retsu* |
| quick | 早い | *Hayai* |
| quickly | 早く | *Hayaku* |
| quiet | 静か | *Shizuka* |
| quite | まったく | *Mattaku* |
| quiz | クイズ | *Kuizu* |

## R

| radio | ラジオ | *Rajio* |
|---|---|---|
| rain | 雨 | *Ame* |
| rape | 強姦 | *Gōkan* |

| **raw** | 生 | **Nama** |
|---|---|---|

*Nama* means "raw" or "uncooked", but it is also means "live" in the sense of live music (*nama no ongaku*).

| ready | 用意ができた | *Yōi ga dekita* |
|---|---|---|
| real | 本物 | *Honmono* |
| receipt | 領収書 | *Ryōshūsho* |
| receipt (shopping) | レシート | *Reshīto* |
| reception | 受付 | *Uketsuke* |
| receptionist | 受付係り | *Uketsuke kakari* |
| red lantern | 赤ちょうちん | *Aka chōchin* |
| reduction | 割引 | *Waribiki* |
| refund | 返済 | *Hensai* |
| to refund | 返済（する） | *Hensai (suru) shimasu* |
| to relax (take a rest) | 休む | *Yasumu* |
| rent (for accommodation) | 家賃 | *Yachin* |
| to rent | (借りる) 借ります | *(Kariru) karimasu* |
| repair | 修理 | *Shuri* |
| reservation | 予約 | *Yoyaku* |
| retired | 退職した | *Taishoku shita* |
| rich | お金持ち | *Okanemochi* |
| road | 道路 | *Dōro* |
| room | 部屋 | *Heya* |
| route | 路線 | *Rosen* |
| rude | 失礼な | *Shitsureina* |
| ruins | 遺跡 | *Iseki* |
| to run | 走る | *Hashiru* |

## S

| safe (deposit box) | 金庫 | *Kinko* |
|---|---|---|

| safe (out of danger) | 安全 | Anzen |
| sauna | サウナ | Sauna |
| Scotland | スコットランド | Sukottorando |
| Scottish | スコットランドの | Sukottorando jin |
| sea | 海 | Umi |
| seat | 席 | Seki |
| seat belt | シートベルト | Shīto beruto |
| sedative | 鎮静剤 | Chin sei zai |
| see you later! | 後で会おう！ | Atode aou! |
| self-service | セルフサービス | Serufu sābisu |
| September | 九月 | Ku gatsu |
| service | サービス | Sābisu |
| shop | 店/…屋 | Mise/...ya |
| to shop | 買い物（する）します | Kaimono (suru) shimasu |
| shopping | 買い物 | Kaimono |
| shopping centre | ショッピングセンター | Shoppingu sentā |
| short | 短い | Mijikai |
| to show | (見せる) 見せます | (Miseru) misemasu |
| shut | (閉める) 閉めます | (Shimeru) shimemasu |
| sign (v) | 署名（する）します | Shomei (suru) shimasu |
|  | サイン（する）します | Sain (suru) shimasu |
| signature | 署名 | Shomei |
| since ... | … から | ... kara |
| sister (elder) | 姉 | Ane |
| sister (younger) | 妹 | Imōto |
| ski | スキー | Sukī |
| sleeping pill | 睡眠薬 | Suimin yaku |
| slow | 遅い | Osoi |
| small | 小さい | Chīsai |
| soft | 柔らかい | Yawarakai |
| some ... | 少しの … | Sukoshi no ... |
| something | 何か | Nani ka |
| son | 息子 | Musuko |
| soon | すぐ | Sugu |
| south | 南 | Minami |
| South Africa | 南アフリカ | Minami Afurika |
| South African | 南アフリカ人 | Minami Afurika jin |
| (at) speed | 急いで | Isoide |
| sport | スポーツ | Supōtsu |
| stadium | スタジアム | Sutajiamu |
| staff | スタッフ | Sutaffu |
| stamp | 切手 | Kitte |
| station | 駅 | Eki |
| sterling (pound) | ポンド | Pondo |
| straight | 真っ直ぐ | Massugu |
| street | 街路/通り | Gairo/doori |
| stress | ストレス | Sutoresu |

| suit | 背広 | *Sebiro* |
|------|------|----------|

*Sebiro*, the traditional word for a man's suit in Japan, stems from the *katakana* pronunciation of "Saville Row".

| suitcase | スーツケース | *Sūtsukēsu* |
|----------|-------------|-------------|
| sun | 太陽 | *Taiyō* |
| sunglasses | サングラス | *Sangurasu* |
| surname | 名字 | *Myōji* |
| swimming pool | プール | *Pūru* |
| symptom | 症状 | *Shōjō* |

### T

| table | テーブル | *Tēburu* |
|-------|----------|----------|
| to take | 取る | *Toru* |
| tampons | タンポン | *Tanpon* |
| tax | 関税 | *Kanzei* |
| tax free | 免税 | *Menzei* |
| taxi | タクシー | *Takushī* |
| telephone | 電話 | *Denwa* |
| telephone box | (公衆) 電話ボックス | *(Kōshū) denwa bokksu* |
| television | テレビ | *Terebi* |
| temple | お寺 | *Otera* |
| tennis | テニス | *Tenisu* |
| tennis court | テニスコート | *Tenisu kōto* |
| to text | メールを (送る) 送ります | *Mēru o (okuru) okurimasu* |

| thank you | どうも | *Dōmo* |
|-----------|--------|--------|

*Dōmo* can be a casual thank you; or it can mean "somehow", as in the expression *dōmo okashii*, "it is somewhat odd".

| that | あれ | *Are* |
|------|------|-------|
| theft | 盗難 | *Tōnan* |
| then (at that time) | その時 | *Sono toki* |
| there | そこ | *Soko* |
| thing | 物 | *Mono* |
| to think | (考える) 考えます | *(Kangaeru) kangaemasu* |
| thirsty | 喉が渇いています | *Nodo ga kawaite imasu* |
| this | これ | *Kore* |
| three | 三 | *San/mitsu* |
| ticket (bus) | バスの切符 | *Basu no kippu* |
| ticket (cinema) | 映画の切符 | *Eiga no kippu* |
| ticket (parking) | 駐車違反カード | *Chūsha ihan kādo* |
| ticket office | 切符売場 | *Kippu uriba* |

| time (clock) | 時間 | *Jikan* |
| timetable | 時刻表 | *jikokuhyō* |
| tip (money) | チップ | *Tippu* |
| tired | 疲れました | *Tsukaremashita* |
| to (go to ...) | … へ/に | *... e/ni* |
| to (the left/right) | へ（左/右へ） | *E (hidari/migi e)* |
| today | 今日 | *Kyō* |
| toilet | トイレ | *Toire* |
| toiletries | 化粧用品 | *Keshō yōhin* |
| toll | 通行税 | *Tsūkōzei* |
| tomorrow | 明日 | *Ashita* |
| tonight | 今晩 | *Kon ban* |
| too ... | もう … | *mō ...* |
| tourist office | 観光案内所 | *Kankō annai jo* |
| town | 町 | *Machi* |
| train | 電車 | *Densha* |
| tram | 市街電車 | *Shigai densha* |
| to translate | 翻訳（する）します | *Honyaku (suru) shimasu* |
| to travel | 旅行（する）します | *Ryokō (suru) shimasu* |
| travel agency | 旅行代理店 | *Ryokō dairi ten* |
| true | 本当 | *Hontō* |
| typhoon | 台風 | *Taifū* |
| typical | 典型的な | *Tenkeitekina* |

### U

| ulcer | 潰瘍 | *Kaiyō* |
| umbrella | 傘 | *Kasa* |
| unconscious | 意識不明の | *Ishiki fumei no* |
| under | … の下 | *... no shita* |
| underground (tube) | 地下鉄 | *Chikatetsu* |
| to understand | (分かる) 分かります | *(Wakaru) wakarimasu* |
| underwear | 下着 | *Shitagi* |
| unemployment | 失業 | *Shitsugyō* |
| unpleasant ... | いやな … | *Iyana ...* |
| upstairs | 上階にある/いる | *Jōkai ni aru/iru* |
| urgent | 緊急 | *Kinkyū* |
| to use | (使う) 使います | *(Tsukau) tsukaimasu* |
| useful | 便利 | *Benri* |
| usually | たいてい | *Taitei* |

### V

| vacant (seat, eg) | あいている | *Aite iru* |
| vacation | 休暇 | *Kyūka* |
| vaccination | 予防接種 | *Yobō sesshu* |
| valid | 有効 | *Yūkō* |
| valuables | 貴重品 | *Kichōhin* |
| value | 価値 | *Kachi* |

| VAT | 消費税 | *Shōhizei* |
|---|---|---|

There is a five per cent non-refundable consumption tax on everything you pay for in Japan.

| | | |
|---|---|---|
| vegetarian | ベジタリアン | *Bejitarian* |
| vehicle | 乗り物 | *Norimono* |
| very | たいへん | *Very* |
| visa | ビザ | *Biza* |
| visit | 訪問 | *Hōmon* |
| to visit | 訪問（する）します | *Hōmon (suru) shimasu* |
| vitamin | ビタミン | *Bitamin* |
| to vomit | (吐く) 吐きます | *(Haku) hakimasu* |

**W**

| | | |
|---|---|---|
| waiter/waitress | ウエーター/ウエートレス | *Uētā/uētoresu* |
| waiting room | 待合室 | *Machiai shitsu* |
| Wales | ウェールズ | *Uēruzu* |
| to walk | (歩く) 歩きます | *(Aruku) arukimasu* |
| wallet | 財布 | *Saifu* |
| to want | 望む | *Nozomu* |
| to wash | (洗う) 洗います | *(Arau) araimsu* |
| watch | 時計 | *Tokei* |
| water | 水 | *Mizu* |
| water sports | ウォーター［水上］スポーツ | *Wōtā/suijō supōtsu* |
| way (manner) | 方法 | *Hōhō* |
| way (route) | 道 | *Michi* |
| way in | 入口 | *Iriguchi* |
| way out | 出口 | *Deguchi* |
| weather | 天気 | *Tenki* |
| web | インターネット/ウエブ | *Intānetto/uebu* |
| website | ウエブサイト | *Uebusaito* |
| week | 週 | *Shū* |
| weekday | 平日 | *Heijitsu* |
| weekend | 週末 | *Shūmatsu* |
| welcome | 歓迎 | *Kangei* |
| well | じょうずに | *Jōzuni* |
| Welsh | ウェールズ人 | *Uēruzu jin* |
| west | 西 | *Nishi* |
| what | 何 | *Nani* |
| wheelchair | 車椅子 | *Kuruma isu* |
| when | いつ | *Itsu* |
| where | どこ | *Doko* |
| which | どちら/どれ/どの | *Dochira/dore/dono* |
| while | しばらく | *Shibaraku* |
| who | だれ | *Dare* |
| why | なぜ/どうして | *Naze/dōshite* |

| wife (my/ someone else's) | 家内/奥さん | *Kanai/okusan* |
| wine | ワイン | *Wain* |
| with | と/一緒に | *To/issho ni* |
| without | … なし | *... nashi* |
| woman | 女の人/女性 | *Onna no hito/josei* |
| wonderful | 素晴らしい | *subarasī* |
| word | 単語 | *Tango* |
| work | 仕事 | *Shigoto* |
| to work (machine) | (動く) 動きます | *(Ugoku) ugokimasu* |
| to work (person) | (働く) 働きます | *(Hataraku) hatarakimasu* |
| world | 世界 | *Sekai* |
| worried | 困っている/います | *Komatte iru/imasu* |
| to write | (書く) 書きます | *(Kaku) kakimasu* |
| wrong (mistaken) | 間違った | *Machigatta* |

### X

| x-ray | レントゲン写真 | *Rentogen shashin* |
| to x-ray | レントゲン写真を (とる)とります | *Rentogen shashin o (toru) torimasu* |

### Y

| yacht | ヨット | *Yotto* |
| year | 年 | *Nen* |
| yearly | 一年一度 | *Ichi nen ichi do* |
| yellow pages | 職業別電話帳 | *Shokugyō betsu denwa chō* |
| yes | はい | *Hai* |
| yesterday | 昨日 | *Kinō* |
| yet | まだ | *Mada* |
| you (formal) | あなた | *Anata* |
| you (informal) | きみ | *Kimi* |
| young | 若い | *Wakai* |
| your (formal) | あなたの | *Anata no* |
| your (informal) | きみの | *Kimi no* |
| youth hostel | ユースホステル | *Yūsuhosuteru* |

### Z

| **zebra crossing** | 横断歩道 | ***Ōdanhodō*** |

Drivers are obliged to stop at *ōdanhodō*, but it is safer to wait for the vehicle to actually stop before crossing.

| zero | ゼロ | *Zero* |
| zone | 地帯 | *Chitai* |
| zoo | 動物園 | *Dōbutsuen* |

# Japanese-English dictionary

## A

| | | |
|---|---|---|
| *Airurando* | アイルランド | Ireland |
| *Airurando jin* | アイルランド人 | Irish |
| *Aite (iru) imasu* | 開いて（いる）います | open |
| *Aite iru* | あいている | vacant (seat,eg) |
| *Aka chōchin* | 赤ちょうちん | red lantern |
| *Akachan* | 赤ちゃん | baby |
| *(Akeru) akemasu* | （開ける）開けます | to open |

| | | |
|---|---|---|
| *Amai* | 甘い | **sweet** |

*Amai* means "sweet" or "sugary in taste or fragrance", but it also means "lenient and lackadaisical" (so easily tricked).

| | | |
|---|---|---|
| *Ame* | 雨 | rain |
| *Amerika* | アメリカ | America |
| *Amerika jin* | アメリカ人 | American (person) |
| *Amerika no ...* | アメリカの … | American ... (car, food, etc.) |
| *Anata* | あなた | you (formal) |
| *Anata no* | あなたの | your (formal) |
| *Ane* | 姉 | sister (one's elder) |
| *Ani* | 兄 | brother (one's elder) |
| *Anzen* | 安全 | safe (out of danger) |
| *Apāto* | アパート | apartment |
| *(Arau) araimsu* | （洗う）洗います | to wash |
| *Are* | あれ | that |
| *Arerugī* | アレルギー | allergy |
| *(Aru) arimasu* | （ある）あります | to be (for inanimate objects) |
| *(Aruku) arukimasu* | （歩く）歩きます | to walk |
| *Ashita* | 明日 | tomorrow |
| *Asupirin* | アスピリン | aspirin |
| *Atarashii* | 新しい | new |
| *Atode aou!* | 後で会おう！ | see you later! |
| *Atsui* | 暑い | hot |

## B

| | | |
|---|---|---|
| *Bā* | バー | bar (pub) |
| *Basho* | 場所 | place |
| *Basu* | バス | bus |
| *Basu no kippu* | バスの切符 | ticket (bus) |
| *Bejitarian* | ベジタリアン | vegetarian |
| *Bengoshi* | 弁護士 | lawyer |
| *Benri* | 便利 | useful |
| *Bin* | 便 | flight |
| *Bitamin* | ビタミン | vitamin |
| *Biyouin* | 美容院 | hairdresser's |
| *Biza* | ビザ | visa |

| Buchō | 部長 | manager |
| Buttai | 物体 | object |
| Byōin | 病院 | hospital |
| Byōki | 病気 | ill |

## C

| Chekku | チェック | cheque |
| Chekku in (suru) shimasu | チェックイン(する) します | to check in (hotel, airport) |
| Chien | 遅延 | delay (n) |
| Chihō | 地方 | area |
| Chiisai | 小さい | little |
| Chikai | 近い | close by/near |
| Chikatetsu | 地下鉄 | underground (tube) |
| Chiku | 地区 | district |
| Chin sei zai | 鎮静剤 | sedative |
| Chintsū zai | 鎮痛剤 | painkiller |
| Chīsai | 小さい | small |
| Chitai | 地帯 | zone |
| Chizu | 地図 | map (city) |
| Chizu | 地図 | map (road) |
| Chōdo | ちょうど | exactly |
| Chokusetsu | 直接 | immediately |
| Chūsha | 駐車 | parking |
| Chūsha ihan kādo | 駐車違反カード | ticket (parking) |
| Chūshin | 中心 | centre |

## D

| Daburu | ダブル | double |
| Daijōbu | 大丈夫 | all right |
| Daijōbu | 大丈夫 | ok |
| Daiseidō | 大聖堂 | cathedral |
| ... dake | … だけ | just (only) |
| Dansei yo toire | 男性用トイレ | gents (toilets) |
| Dare? | だれ? | who? |
| Dassui (suru) shimasu | 脱水（する）します | to dehydrate |
| ... de | … で | by (via) |
| Deguchi | 出口 | exit/way out |
| (Dekiru) dekimasu | (できる) できます | can (to be able) |
| Dengon | 伝言 | message |
| Densensei | 伝染性 | contagious |
| Densha | 電車 | train |
| Denshi mēru | 電子メール | e-mail |
| Denwa | 電話 | telephone |
| Denwa (suru) shimasu | 電話（する）します | to call |
| Denwa o (kakeru) kakemasu | 電話を（かける）かけます | to dial |
| Dō/dore/dono | どう/どれ/どの | how |
| Dōbutsuen | 動物園 | zoo |
| Dochira/dore/dono | どちら/どれ/どの | which |

| *Doko* | どこ | where |
| *Dokomo ... nai* | どこも … ない | nowhere |
| *Dono gurai kakarimasu ka?* | どのぐらいかかりますか？ | how far (how long does it take)? |
| *Doraikurīnigu (suru) shimasu* | ドライクリーニング（する）します | to dry clean |
| *Doraikurīningu ten* | ドライクリーニング店 | dry cleaner's |
| *Dōro* | 道路 | road |
| *Dōshite?* | どうして？ | why? |

E

| *E (hidari/migi e)* | へ（左/右へ） | to (the left/right) |
| *... e* | …へ | to (go to ...) |
| *Eiga* | 映画 | film (cinema) |
| *Eiga no kippu* | 映画の切符 | ticket (cinema) |
| *Eigakan* | 映画館 | cinema |
| *Eigo* | 英語 | English |
| *Eizu* | エイズ | AIDS |
| *Eki* | 駅 | station |
| *Erabu* | 選ぶ | to choose |
| *Erebētā* | エレベーター | lift |

F

| *Firumu* | フィルム | film (camera) |
| *Fuku* | 服 | clothes |
| *Futari* | ふたり | a pair (couple) |

G

| *Gaido* | ガイド | guide |

| **Gaikoku jin/gaijin** | 外国人/外人 | **foreigner** |
| --- | --- | --- |

**Pin back those lug-holes:** *gaijin* is a word you are likely to hear a lot while you are in Japan.

| *Gairo/doori* | 街路/通り | street |
| *Gasorin* | ガソリン | petrol |
| *Gasorin sutando* | ガソリンスタンド | petrol station |
| *Gasu* | ガス | gas |
| *Geijutsu* | 芸術 | art |
| *Gengo* | 言語 | language |
| *genkan* | 玄関 | front door |
| *Genkin* | 現金 | cash (n) |
| *Go gatsu* | 五月 | May |
| *Gōkan* | 強姦 | rape |
| *... goro (rokuji goro)* | …ごろ（六時ごろ） | Around ... (Around six o' clock) |
| *Gorufu* | ゴルフ | golf |
| *Gorufu jō* | ゴルフ場 | golf course |
| *Gurūpu* | グループ | group |
| *Gyararī* | ギャラリー | gallery |

# H

| | | |
|---|---|---|
| *Hachi gatsu* | 八月 | August |
| *Haha/okāsan* | 母/お母さん | own/someone else's mother |
| *Hai* | はい | yes |
| *(Haku) hakimasu* | (吐く) 吐きます | to vomit |
| *Hakubutsukan* | 博物館 | museum |
| *Hamaki* | 葉巻 | cigar |

| *Hanami* | 花見 | cherry blossom viewing |
|---|---|---|

The romantic perception of *hanami* is that people gather underneath the cherry trees and and wax lyrical as blossoms fall. The reality is a more of a raucous, drunken orgy centred around open-air karaoke.

| | | |
|---|---|---|
| *Hanarete* | 離れて | away |
| *Hanbun* | 半分 | half |
| *Hanzai* | 犯罪 | crime |
| *(Hashiru) hashirimashita* | (走る) 走りました | to run |
| *(Hataraku) hatarakimasu* | (働く) 働きます | to work (person) |
| *Hayai* | 早い | early |
| *Hayai* | 早い | quick |
| *Hayaku* | 早く | quickly |
| *Heijitsu* | 平日 | weekday |
| *Heikan* | 閉館 | closed |
| *Hensai* | 返済 | refund |
| *Hensai (suru) shimasu* | 返済 (する) | to refund |
| *Heya* | 部屋 | room |
| *Hi* | 日 | day |
| *Higai* | 被害 | damage (n) |
| *Hijō guchi* | 非常口 | fire exit |
| *Hikōki* | 飛行機 | aeroplane |
| *Hiruma* | 昼間 | midday |
| *Hito* | 人 | person |
| *Hito bito* | 人々 | people |
| *Hitsuyō* | 必要 | necessary |
| *Hiyō* | 費用 | cost |
| *Hōhō* | 方法 | way (manner) |
| *Hoka no* | 他の | other |
| *Hoken* | 保険 | insurance |
| *Hōkō* | 方向 | directions |
| *Hōmon* | 訪問 | visit |
| *Hōmon (suru) shimasu* | 訪問 (する) します | to visit |
| *Homosekushal* | ホモセクシャル | homosexual |
| *Hon* | 本 | book |
| *honmono* | 本物 | real |
| *Hontō* | 本当 | true |

| | | |
|---|---|---|
| *Honyaku (suru) shimasu* | 翻訳（する）します | to translate |
| *Hoshō* | 保証 | guarantee |
| *Hoteru* | ホテル | hotel |

**I**

| | | |
|---|---|---|
| *Ich do mo ... nai* | 一度も …. ない | never |
| *Ichi ban (ooku)* | 一番（多く） | most |
| *Ichi ban sukina ...* | いちばん好きな … | favourite |
| *Ichi do* | 一度 | once |
| *Ichi gatsu* | 一月 | January |
| *Ichi nen ichi do* | 一年一度 | yearly |
| *Ichiba* | 市場 | market |
| *Ichiban ii* | 一番いい | best |
| *Igirisu* | イギリス | England |
| *Ii (hito)* | いい（人） | nice (people) |
| *Ikura desu ka?* | いくらですか？ | how much? |
| *Ima* | 今 | now |
| *Imōto* | 妹 | sister (one's younger) |
| *Inaka* | 田舎 | countryside |
| *Inakunaru* | いなくなる | missing |
| *Infuruenza* | インフルエンザ | flu |
| *Intānetto/uebu* | インターネット/ウエブ | Internet/web |
| *Iriguchi* | 入口 | entrance/way in |
| *Iro* | 色 | colour |
| *Iru* | 居る | to be (for living things) |
| *Iseki* | 遺跡 | ruins |
| *Isha* | 医者 | doctor |
| *Ishiki fumei no* | 意識不明の | unconscious |
| *Isoide/Isoide!* | 急いで/急いで！ | (at) speed/hurry up! |
| *Itsu* | いつ | when? |
| *Iyana ...* | いやな … | unpleasant ... |

**J**

| | | |
|---|---|---|
| *Jetto sukī* | ジェット スキー | jet ski |
| *Jikan* | 時間 | time (clock) |
| *Jikokuhyō* | 時刻表 | timetable |
| *Jimoto no* | 地元の | local |

| | | |
|---|---|---|
| **Jitensha** | 自転車 | **bicycle** |

**Bicycles are a health hazard in Japan. The roads are dangerous so cyclists tend to ride on the footpath!**

| | | |
|---|---|---|
| *Jiyū* | 自由 | free |
| *Jōhō* | 情報 | information |
| *Jōkai ni aru/iru* | 上階にある/いる | upstairs |
| *Josei yo toire* | 女性用トイレ | ladies (toilets) |
| *Jōzuni* | じょうずに | well |
| *Jūbun* | 十分 | enough |
| *Jūgatsu* | 十月 | October |
| *Jūichi gatsu* | 十一月 | November |
| *Junbi suru* | 準備する | to arrange |

| | | |
|---|---|---|
| *Jūni gatsu* | 十二月 | December |

**K**

| | | |
|---|---|---|
| *Ka* | 蚊 | mosquito |
| *... kara* | …から | because ... |
| *Kachi* | 価値 | value |
| *Kādo de (harau) haraimasu* | カードで（はらう）払います | to charge (credit card) |
| *Kagi* | 鍵 | key |
| *Kaigan* | 海岸 | coast |
| *Kaigan/bīchi* | 海岸/ビーチ | beach |
| *Kaigi* | 会議 | meeting |
| *Kaimono* | 買い物 | shopping |
| *Kaimono (suru) shimasu* | 買い物（する）します | to shop |
| *Kaiwahyōgen shū* | 会話表現集 | phrase book |
| *Kaiyō* | 潰瘍 | ulcer |
| *Kaji* | 火事 | fire |
| *Kajino* | カジノ | casino |
| *kakarimasu* | かかります | to cost |
| *(Kaku) kakimasu* | （書く）書きます | to write |
| *Kakunin (suru) shimasu* | 確認（する）します | to confirm |
| *Kakushō* | 確証 | confirmation |
| *Kamera* | カメラ | camera |
| *Kami* | 髪 | hair |
| *Kanai/okusan* | 家内/奥さん | (my) wife/(your) wife |
| *(Kangaeru) kangaemasu* | （考える）/考えます | to think |
| *Kangei* | 歓迎 | welcome |
| *Kānibaru* | カーニバル | carnival |
| *Kanjō* | 勘定 | bill |
| *Kankin (suru) shimasu* | 換金（する）します | to cash |
| *Kankō annai jo* | 観光案内所 | tourist office |
| *Kanōna* | 可能な | possible |
| *Kanpai* | 乾杯 | cheers (toast) |
| *Kanzei* | 関税 | duty (tax) |
| *Kanzei* | 関税 | tax |
| *Kara* | から | from |
| *... kara* | …から | because .../since ... |
| *(Kariru) karimasu* | （借りる）借ります | to rent |
| *Kasa* | 傘 | umbrella |
| *Katto (suru) shimasu* | カット（する）します | to cut |
| *(Kau) kaimasu* | （買う）買います | to buy |
| *Kawase rēto* | 為替レート | exchange rate |
| *Keisatsu* | 警察 | police |
| *Keitai denwa* | 携帯電話 | mobile phone |
| *Kekkon shite (iru) imasu* | 結婚して（いる）います | married |
| *Keshō yōhin* | 化粧用品 | toiletries |
| *(Kigaeru) kigaemasu* | 着替える | to change (one's clothes) |

| | | |
|---|---|---|
| *Kī horudā* | キーホルダー | key ring |
| *Kībōdo* | キーボード | keyboard |
| *Kichōhin* | 貴重品 | valuables |
| *Kiken* | 危険 | danger |
| *Kimi* | きみ | you (informal) |
| *Kimi no* | きみの | your (informal) |
| *Kinko* | 金庫 | safe (deposit box) |
| *Kinkyū* | 緊急 | emergency |
| *Kinkyū* | 緊急 | urgent |
| *Kinnenbi* | 記念日 | anniversary |
| *Kinō* | 昨日 | yesterday |
| *Kiosuku* | キオスク | kiosk |
| *Kippu uriba* | 切符売場 | box office/ticket office |
| *Kirete (iru) imasu* | 切れて（いる）います | off (switched) |
| *Kissaten* | 喫茶店 | café/coffee house |
| *Kisu* | キス | kiss |
| *Kita* | 北 | north |
| *Kitanai* | 汚い | dirty |
| *Kitte* | 切手 | stamp |
| *Kizu* | 傷 | cut (wound) |
| *... ko* | … 湖 | Lake ... |

| | | |
|---|---|---|
| **Kōban** | 交番 | **police box** |

**There are *kōban* in strategic places all over Japan, from which the police can keep an eye on things.**

| | | |
|---|---|---|
| *Kodomo* | 子供 | child |
| *Kōen* | 公園 | park |
| *Koin randrī* | コインランドリー | launderette |
| *Kojinteki na* | 個人的な | private |
| *Koko* | ここ | here |
| *Kōkūbin* | 航空便 | airmail |
| *Kokusai* | 国際 | international |
| *Kokuseki* | 国籍 | nationality |
| *Kōkyō kōtsū kikan* | 公共交通機関 | public transport |
| *Komatte iru/imasu* | 困っている/います | worried |
| *Kon ban* | 今晩 | tonight |
| *Konpyūta* | コンピュータ | computer |
| *Kore* | これ | this |
| *Kōsaten* | 交差点 | junction |
| *Koshō* | 故障 | out of order |
| *(Kōshū) denwa bokksu* | (公衆) 電話ボックス | telephone box |
| *(Kotaeru) kotaemasu* | (答える) 答えます | to answer |
| *Kōtsū densha* | 交通電車 | railway |
| *Kōtsū jiko* | 交通事故 | accident (traffic) |
| *(Kowasu) kowashimasu* | (壊す) 壊します | to damage |
| *Ku gatsu* | 九月 | September |
| *Kuizu* | クイズ | quiz |
| *Kūkō* | 空港 | airport |

| | | |
|---|---|---|
| *Kuni* | 国 | country |
| *Kurabu* | クラブ | club |
| *Kurejitto kādo* | クレジットカード | credit card |
| *Kurīmu* | クリーム | cream |
| *Kuruma* | 車 | car |
| *Kuruma isu* | 車椅子 | wheelchair |
| *Kyanseru (suru) shimasu* | キャンセル（する）します | to cancel |
| *Kyasshu kōnā* | キャッシュコーナー | cash point |
| *Kyō* | 今日 | today |
| *Kyūjitsu* | 休日 | holiday (work-free day) |
| *Kyūka* | 休暇 | holidays/vacation |
| *Kyūkō* | 急行 | express (train) |
| *Kyūkyūsha* | 救急車 | ambulance |
| *Kyūmei dōi* | 救命胴衣 | life jacket |

## M

| | | |
|---|---|---|
| *Machi* | 町 | town |
| *Machiai shitsu* | 待合室 | waiting room |
| *Machigai* | 間違い | error |
| *Machigatta* | 間違った | wrong (mistaken) |
| *Mada* | まだ | yet |
| *... mae* | … 前 | ... ago |
| *Manshon* | マンション | apartment |
| *Massugu* | 真っ直ぐ | straight |
| *Mattaku* | まったく | quite |
| *Matsuri* | 祭 | festivals |
| *Mayaku* | 麻薬 | drug |
| *Mayonaka* | 真夜中 | midnight |
| *Megane* | めがね | glasses |
| *Megane ya* | 眼鏡屋 | optician's |

| | | |
|---|---|---|
| ***Meishi*** | 名刺 | **business card** |

**Most Japanese carry business cards to give out whenever they meet someone for the first time.**

| | | |
|---|---|---|
| *Menzei* | 免税 | tax free |
| *Mēru o (okuru) okurimasu* | メールを（送る）送ります | to text |
| *Mezamashi dokei* | 目覚まし時計 | alarm (clock) |
| *Mibun shōmeisyo* | 身分証明書 | identity card |
| *Michi* | 道 | way (route) |
| *Mijikai* | 短い | short |
| *Minami* | 南 | south |
| *Minami Afurika* | 南アフリカ | South Africa |
| *Minami Afurika jin* | 南アフリカ人 | South African |
| *Minato* | 港 | port (sea) |
| *Minna no* | 皆の | all |
| *Mise/...ya* | 店/…屋 | shop (n) |
| *(Miseru) misemasu* | （見せる）見せます | to show |
| *Mizu* | 水 | water |
| *Mizuumi* | 湖 | lake |

| *mo ...* | も … | and |
| *... mō ...* | … もう … | ... too ... |
| *Mō ichi do* | もう一度 | again |
| *Mochinushi* | 持ち主 | owner |
| *Mondai* | 問題 | problem |
| *Monku* | 文句 | complaint |
| *Monku o (iu) iimasu* | 文句を（言う） いいます | to complain |
| *Mono* | 物 | thing |
| *Motto* | もっと | more |
| *Motto ii* | もっといい | better |
| *Mukai* | 向かい | opposite (place) |
| *Muryō* | 無料 | free (money) |
| *Musuko* | 息子 | son |
| *Musume* | 娘 | daughter |
| *Muzukashii* | 難しい | difficult |
| *Myōji* | 名字 | surname |
| *Myūjikaru* | ミュージカル | musical (show) |

### N

| *Nagasa wa dore kurai desu ka?* | 長さはどれぐらい ですか？ | how long (length)? |
| *Naito kurabu* | ナイトクラブ | nightclub |
| *Naka* | 中 | inside |
| *Namae* | 名前 | name |
| *(Nakusu) nakushimasu* | （なくす）なくします | to lose |
| *Nani?* | 何？ | what? |
| *Nani ka* | 何か | something |
| *Nanimo … nai* | なにも … ない | nothing |
| *... nashi* | … なし | without |
| *Naze?* | なぜ？ | why? |
| *Nedan* | 値段 | price |
| *Nen* | 年 | year |
| *Netsu* | 熱 | heat |
| *... ni ...* | … に …, | and |
| *... ni* | … に | at (time) |
| *... ni* | … へ | to (go to ...) |
| *Ni gatsu* | 二月 | February |
| *Ni tsuite* | について | about (concerning) |
| *Nimotsu* | 荷物 | baggage/luggage |

| ***Ningyō*** | 人形 | **doll** |

**Dolls are made all over Japan as works of art, ornaments or toys in a variety of styles and materials.**

| *Nishi* | 西 | west |
| *No aida* | の間 | between |
| *No aida* | の間 | during |
| *... no naka ni* | の中に | in |
| *... no retsu* | … の列 | queue |
| *... no shita* | … の下 | under |

| ... no soba ni | … のそばに | by (beside) |
| ... no sugu soba ni | … のすぐそばに | next to |
| ... no tame ni | … のために… | because of ... |
| ... no tame ni | … のために | for ... (in order to) |
| ... no ue | … の上 | on |
| Nodo ga kawaite imasu | 喉が渇いています | thirsty |
| (Norikaeru) norikaemasu | (乗り換える) 乗り換えます | to change (trains, etc.) |
| Norimono | 乗り物 | vehicle |
| (Nozomu) nozomimasu | (望む) 望みます | to want |
| Nyūsu | ニュース | news |

O

| Ōdanhodō | 横断歩道 | zebra crossing |
| Ofisu/eigyō sho | オフィス/営業所 | office |
| Ofuro | お風呂 | bath |
| Ojama shimasu | おじゃまします | to disturb |
| Okane | お金 | money |
| Okanemochi | お金持ち | rich |
| Ōki | 大きい | big |
| Okugai | 屋外 | outdoor |
| Okureta | 遅れた | late (delayed) |
| Okusama | 奥様 | madam |
| Okyaku san | お客さん | customer |
| Okyūteate | 応急手当 | first aid |
| Omona | 主な | main |
| Omoshiroi | 面白い | interesting |
| Onna no hito/josei | 女の人/女性 | woman |
| Onna no hito | 女のひと | lady |
| Onna no ko | 女の子 | girl |
| Ookisa wa dore gurai desu ka? | 大きさはどれぐらいですか？ | how big? |
| Operētā | オペレーター | operator |
| Oritatami shiki beddo | 折りたたみ式ベッド | cot |
| Osatsu | お札 | note (money) |

| **Oshiro** | お城 | **castle** |

Japanese castles are magnificent structures that evolved in the *Sengoku* (Warring States) era from about 1500 to 1600.

| Osoi | 遅い | late (time) |
| Osoi | 遅い | slow |
| Ōsutoraria | オーストラリア | Australia |
| Ōsutoraria jin | オーストラリア人 | Australian |
| Otera | お寺 | temple |
| Otoko no hito | 男の人 | man |
| Otoko no ko | 男の子 | boy |
| Otō-san | お父さん | father |
| Otōto | 弟 | brother (younger) |

| ... oyobi | …および | and |

| Pabu | パブ | pub |

| *Pachinko* | パチンコ | **pachinko** |

The most popular form of entertainment in Japan, *pachinko* is a kind of high-tech pinball that pays out prizes.

| Pasupōto | パスポート | passport |
| Pātī | パーティー | party |
| Pondo | ポンド | sterling pound |
| Pun/fun | 分 | minute |
| Purattohōmu | プラットホーム | platform |
| Pūru | プール | swimming pool |

| Raberu | ラベル | label |
| Raifu gādo | ライフガード | lifeguard |
| Rajio | ラジオ | radio |
| Renraku (suru) shimasu | 連絡（する）します | to contact |
| Rentogen shashin | レントゲン写真 | x-ray |
| Rentogen shashin o (toru) torimasu | レントゲン写真を（とる）とります | to x-ray |
| Reshīto | レシート | receipt (shopping) |
| Roku gatsu | 六月 | June |
| Rosen | 路線 | route |
| Ryōgae (suru) shimasu | 両替する（します） | to change (money) |
| Ryōgae ten | 両替店 | bureau de change |
| Ryōjikan | 領事館 | consulate |
| Ryōkin | 料金 | charge |
| Ryokō | 旅行 | journey |
| Ryokō (suru) shimasu | 旅行（する）します | to travel |
| Ryokō dairi ten | 旅行代理店 | travel agency |
| Ryōshin | 両親 | parents |
| Ryōshūsho | 領収書 | receipt |
| Ryotei | 旅程 | itinerary |

| Sābisu | サービス | service |
| Saifu | 財布 | wallet |
| Saigo | 最後 | last |
| Saikuringu | サイクリング | cycling |
| Saitei | 最低 | minimum |
| Sakkā | サッカー | football |
| Sakura | 桜 | cherry blossoms |
| Samui | 寒い | cold (weather) |
| San gatsu | 三月 | March |
| Sangurasu | サングラス | sunglasses |

| | | |
|---|---|---|
| *Sanso* | 酸素 | oxygen |
| *Sauna* | サウナ | sauna |
| *Sebiro* | 背広 | suit (man's) |
| *Sekai* | 世界 | world |
| *Seki* | 席 | seat |
| *Senaka* | 背中 | back (body) |
| *Serufu sābisu* | セルフサービス | self-service |
| *Setsubi* | 設備 | facilities |
| *Shashin* | 写真 | photo |

| **Shi/yon** | **四** | **four** |
|---|---|---|

The number four, *shi*, is considered an unlucky number in Japanese as another word pronounced *shi* (a different *kanji*) is also the word for "death".

| | | |
|---|---|---|
| *Shī Dī* | CD | CD |
| *Shi gatsu* | 四月 | April |
| *Shibaraku* | しばらく | while |
| *Shichi gatsu* | 七月 | July |
| *Shickaku shitsu* | 試着室 | fitting room |
| *Shigai densha* | 市街電車 | tram |
| *Shigai kyokuban* | 市外局番 | area code |
| *Shigoto* | 仕事 | business |
| *Shigoto* | 仕事 | work |
| *Shikashi* | しかし | but |
| *Shima* | 島 | island |
| *Shimbun* | 新聞 | newspaper |
| *(Shimeru)* *shimemasu* | (閉める) 閉めます | to close, shut |
| *(…shinakereba narimasen)* | (…しなければなりません) | must |
| *…shinakereba naranai* | …しなければならない | |
| *Shinsetsu* | 親切 | kind |
| *Shintai shōgai sha* | 身体障害者 | disabled |
| *Shita* | 下 | down |
| *Shitagi* | 下着 | underwear |
| *Shīto beruto* | シートベルト | seat belt |
| *Shitsu* | 質 | quality |
| *Shitsugyō* | 失業 | unemployment |
| *Shitsumon* | 質問 | query |
| *Shitsumon* | 質問 | question |
| *Shitsureina* | 失礼な | rude |
| *Shizuka* | 静か | quiet |
| *Shōhizei* | 消費税 | VAT |
| *Shohōsen* | 処方箋 | prescription |
| *Shōjō* | 症状 | symptom |
| *Shoku chūdoku* | 食中毒 | food poisoning |
| *Shokugyō betsu denwa chō* | 職業別電話帳 | yellow pages |
| *Shomei* | 署名 | signature |

| | | |
|---|---|---|
| *Shomei (suru) shimasu* | 署名（する）します | sign |
| *Sain (suru) shimasu* | サイン（する）します | pledge |
| *Shoppingu sentā* | ショッピングセンター | shopping centre |
| *Shū* | 週 | week |
| *Shujin/goshujin* | 主人/ご主人 | my/someone else's husband |
| *Shukuhaku setsubi* | 宿泊設備 | accommodation |
| *Shūmatsu* | 週末 | weekend |
| *Shunkan* | 瞬間 | moment |
| *Shuri* | 修理 | repair |
| *Shūrikō* | 修理工 | mechanic |
| *Shūrikōjō* | 修理工場 | garage |
| *Shurui* | 種類 | kind (sort) |
| *Soko* | そこ | there |
| *Sokutatsu* | 速達 | express (delivery) |
| *Sono toki* | その時 | then (at that time) |
| *Sōpurando* | ソープランド | massage parlour |
| *Soto* | 外 | outside |
| *Subarasī* | 素晴らしい | wonderful |
| *Sugu* | すぐ | soon |
| *Suimin yaku* | 睡眠薬 | sleeping pill |
| *Sūji* | 数字 | number (figure) |
| *Sukī* | スキー | ski |
| *Suki desu* | 好きです | like |
| *Sukoshi* | 少し | bit (a) |
| *Sukoshi no ...* | 少しの … | some ... |
| *Sukottorando* | スコットランド | Scotland |
| *Sukottorando jin* | スコットランド人 | Scottish |
| *Sukunai* | 少ない | less |
| *Supōtsu* | スポーツ | sport |
| *Sūryō* | 数量 | quantity |
| *Sutaffu* | スタッフ | staff |
| *Sutajiamu* | スタジアム | stadium |
| *Sutekina* | すてきな | nice |
| *Sutoresu* | ストレス | stress |
| *Sūtsukēsu* | スーツケース | suitcase |
| *Suzushī* | 涼しい | cool |

## T

| | | |
|---|---|---|
| *Tabako* | タバコ | cigarette |
| *Tabun* | たぶん | maybe/probably |
| *Tada* | ただ | only |

| | | |
|---|---|---|
| ***Taifū*** | **台風** | **typhoon** |

Typhoons usually hit between late summer and autumn, and are stronger in the south, where they sometimes stop traffic.

| | | |
|---|---|---|
| *Taihen* | たいへん | very |
| *Taisetsu* | 大切 | important |
| *Taishikan* | 大使館 | embassy |

| | | |
|---|---|---|
| *Taishoku shita* | 退職した | retired |
| *Taitei* | たいてい | usually |
| *Taiyō* | 太陽 | sun |
| *Takai* | 高い | high |
| *Takusan* | たくさん | much |
| *Takusan no* | たくさんの | many |
| *Takushī* | タクシー | taxi |
| *Tango* | 単語 | word |
| *Tanpon* | タンポン | tampons |
| *Tasukete!* | 助けて！ | help! |
| *(Tazuneru) tazunemasu* | (尋ねる) 尋ねます | to ask (inquire) |
| *Tēburu* | テーブル | table |
| *Tenisu* | テニス | tennis |
| *Tenisu kōto* | テニスコート | tennis court |
| *Tenkeitekina* | 典型的な | typical |
| *Tenki* | 天気 | weather |
| *Tenrankai* | 展覧会 | exhibition |
| *Terebi* | テレビ | television |
| *... to ...* | … と …, | and |
| *Tippu* | チップ | tip (money) |
| *To/issho ni* | と/一緒に | with |
| *Tōchaku* | 到着 | arrival |
| *Toire* | トイレ | toilet |
| *Tōjōken* | 搭乗券 | boarding card |
| *Tokei* | 時計 | watch |
| *Tomodachi* | 友達 | friend |
| *Tōnan* | 盗難 | theft |
| *Tooi* | 遠い | far |
| *(Toru) torimasu* | (取る) 取ります | to take |
| *Toshi* | 都市 | city |
| *Toshokan* | 図書館 | library |
| *Tsugi* | 次 | next |
| *Tsūka* | 通貨 | currency |
| *Tsukaremashita* | 疲れました | tired |
| *(Tsukau) tsukaimasu* | (使う) 使います | to use |
| *Tsukete imasu* | つけています | switched on |
| *Tsūkōzei* | 通行税 | toll |

### U

| | | |
|---|---|---|
| *Uebusaito* | ウエブサイト | website |
| *Uēruzu* | ウェールズ | Wales |
| *Uēruzu jin* | ウェールズの | Welsh |
| *Uētā/uētoresu* | ウエーター/ウエートレス | waiter/waitress |
| *(Ugoku) ugokimasu* | (動く) 動きます | to work (machine) |
| *Uketsuke* | 受付 | reception |
| *Uketsuke kakari* | 受付係り | receptionist |
| *Umi* | 海 | sea |
| *Unten (suru) shimasu* | 運転 (する) します | to drive |
| *Unten menkyoshō* | 運転免許証 | driving licence |
| *Untenshu* | 運転手 | driver |
| *Ushiro* | 後ろ | back (place) |

## W

| Wain | わいん | wine |
| Wakai | 若い | young |
| (Wakaru) wakarimasu | (分かる) 分かります | to understand |
| Waribiki | 割引 | discount/reduction |
| Warui | 悪い | bad |
| Wasure mono toriatsukaijo | 忘れ物取扱所 | lost property |
| Watashi no | 私の | my |
| Wōtā/suijō supōtsu | ウォーター［水上］スポーツ | water sports |

## Y

| ... ya ... | …や…, | and |
| ...ya | …屋 | shop (n) |
| Yachin | 家賃 | rent (for accommodation) |
| (Yaku) yakimasu | (焼く) 焼きます | to burn |
| Yasashii | 優しい（人） | kind (person) |
| Yasui | 安い | cheap |
| (Yasumu) yasumimasu | (休む) 休みます | to relax (take a rest) |
| Yawarakai | 柔らかい | soft |
| Yobō sesshu | 予防接種 | vaccination |
| Yodooshi | 夜通し | overnight |
| Yōfuku | 洋服 | clothes (Western) |
| Yōi ga dekita | 用意ができた | ready |
| Yoi/ii | 良い/いい | good |

| **Yopparatta** | 酔っぱらった | **drunk** |

**Public drunkenness is a fairly common sight, but while Japanese drunks can be raucous, they are rarely violent.**

| Yoru | 夜 | night |
| Yōshi | 用紙 | form (document) |
| Yotto | ヨット | yacht |
| Yoyaku | 予約 | appointment |
| Yoyaku | 予約 | booking |
| Yoyaku | 予約 | reservation |
| Yoyaku (suru) shimasu | 予約（する）します | to book |
| Yūbin | 郵便 | post |
| Yūbin butsu | 郵便物 | mail |
| Yūbinkyoku | 郵便局 | post office |
| Yūkō | 有効 | valid |
| Yūsen seki | 優先席 | priority seat (for elderly or disabled) |
| Yūsuhosuteru | ユースホステル | youth hostel |

## Z

| Zeikan | 税関 | customs |
| Zero | ゼロ | zero |

# Quick Reference

## Numbers

| | | |
|---|---|---|
| 0 | ゼロ/零 | *Zero/rei* |
| 1 | 一 | *Ichi* |
| 2 | 二 | *Ni* |
| 3 | 三 | *San* |
| 4 | 四 | *Shi/yon* |
| 5 | 五 | *Go* |
| 6 | 六 | *Roku* |
| 7 | 七 | *Shichi/nana* |
| 8 | 八 | *Hachi* |
| 9 | 九 | *Kyū/ku* |
| 10 | 十 | *Jū* |
| 11 | 十一 | *Jū ichi* |
| 12 | 十二 | *Jū ni* |
| 13 | 十三 | *Jū san* |
| 14 | 十四 | *Jū shi/yon* |
| 15 | 十五 | *Jū go* |
| 16 | 十六 | *Jū roku* |
| 17 | 十七 | *Jū shichi/nana* |
| 18 | 十八 | *Jū hachi* |
| 19 | 十九 | *Jū ku/kyū* |
| 20 | 二十 | *Ni jū* |
| 21 | 二十一 | *Ni jū ichi* |
| 30 | 三十 | *San jū* |
| 40 | 四十 | *Yon jū* |
| 50 | 五十 | *Go jū* |
| 60 | 六十 | *Roku jū* |
| 70 | 七十 | *Nana jū* |
| 80 | 八十 | *Hachi jū* |
| 90 | 九十 | *Kyū jū* |
| 100 | 百 | *Hyaku* |
| 1000 | 一千 | *Issen* |
| 2000 | 二千 | *Nisen* |
| 3000 | 三千 | *Sanzen* |
| | | |
| 1st | 一番 | *Ichi ban* |
| 2nd | 二番 | *Niban* |
| 3rd | 三番 | *Sanban* |
| 4th | 四番 | *Yonban* |
| 5th | 五番 | *Goban* |

# Weights & measures

| gram (=0.03oz) | グラム | *Guramu* |
| kilogram (=2.2lb) | キログラム | *Kiroguramu* |
| centimetre (=0.4in) | センチ | *Senchi* |
| metre (=1.1yd) | メートル | *Mētoru* |
| kilometre (=0.6m) | キロメートル | *Kiromētoru* |
| litre (=2.1pt) | リットル | *Littoru* |

# Days & time

| Monday | 月曜日 | *Getsuyōbi* |
| Tuesday | 火曜日 | *Kayōbi* |
| Wednesday | 水曜日 | *Suiyōbi* |
| Thursday | 木曜日 | *Mokuyōbi* |
| Friday | 金曜日 | *Kinyōbi* |
| Saturday | 土曜日 | *Doyōbi* |
| Sunday | 日曜日 | *Nichiyōbi* |

| What time is it? | 何時ですか？ | *Nan ji desu ka?* |
| (Four) o'clock | (四) 時 | *(Yo) ji* |
| Quarter past (six) | (六時) 十五分 | *(Roku ji) jū go fun* |
| Half past (eight) | (六時) 半 | *(Roku ji) han* |
| Quarter to (ten) | (十時) 十五分前 | *(Jū ji) jū go fun mae* |

| morning | 午前 | *Gozen* |
| afternoon | 午後 | *Gogo* |
| evening | 夕方 | *Yūgata* |
| night | 夜 | *Yoru* |

# Clothes size conversions

| Women's clothes | 7 | 9 | 11 | 13 | 15 | 17 | 19 | 21 |
|---|---|---|---|---|---|---|---|---|
| equiv. UK size | 6 | 8 | 10 | 12 | 14 | 16 | 18 | 20 |

| Men's jackets | S | S | M | L | L | LL | LL | LL |
|---|---|---|---|---|---|---|---|---|
| equiv. UK size | 34 | 36 | 38 | 40 | 42 | 44 | 46 | 48 |

| Men's shirts | 36 | 37 | 38 | 39 | 40 | 41 | 42 | 43 |
|---|---|---|---|---|---|---|---|---|
| equiv. UK size | 14 | 14.5 | 15 | 15.5 | 16 | 16.5 | 17 | 17.5 |

| Shoes | 22.5 | 23.5 | 24.5 | 25.5 | 26.5 | 27.5 | 28.5 | 29.5 |
|---|---|---|---|---|---|---|---|---|
| equiv. UK size | 4 | 5 | 6 | 7 | 8 | 9 | 10 | 11 |